# I DARE YOU

*Finding your passion and lighting your world*

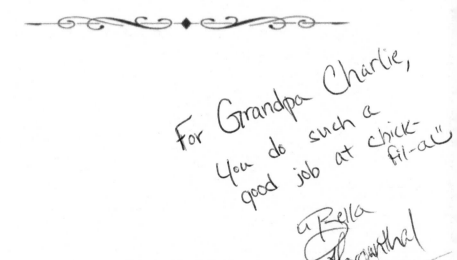

For Grandpa Charlie,
You do such a
good job at chick-
fil-a"

a Bella
Morganthal

phil. 3:7

Isabella D. Morganthal

*I Dare You*

Published by Morganthal Press
*thekingsdaughtermag@gmail.com*
Cover design by BushMaid Design and Isabella D. Morganthal

ISBN # 978-0692437100

*This book is dedicated to my twin sister and best friend, Kenzie. You are changing your world. I love you so much. Thank you for daring me first.*

*And this is also for my Jesus. Where would I be without You, Lord? I love You and will always follow You. You are worth it all!*

*I Dare You*

# Contents

# Introduction

## A Letter For My Readers:

*When I began* the process of writing this book over a year ago, I had no idea that it would turn out this way. I thought that I would write down a few of my thoughts and share it in a few pages. To see it turn into a book a year later is such a joy to my heart.

I have been praying for you as I have written and I wish that I could meet you and pray for you by name.

I am so excited that you have chosen to read this book, so that we can take this journey—this dare—together. You could have chosen to pick up any book out there and you chose this one. I am deeply honored and humbled. Before you begin to read, I just want to let you in on a little secret...

*This isn't my book.*

Yes, technically I wrote it, but it isn't mine. Before I typed one single word I dedicated this book to Jesus Christ and gave it to Him. Whatever comes of it is for His glory and honor alone. To God be all the glory forever!

Now I think it's time that we take a little journey together. I encourage you to do your own praying before we get started. I don't want this dare to be taken lightly. I want it to be the way that I choose to live my life, and I hope you will too.

When you're ready, start to read. Open your heart to what God is speaking to you and dare to dream. Dream of what God wants to do through you when you give everything to Him and the ways that He wants to use you to change this world.

Are you ready for the adventure of your life?


*Your friend,*
*Isabella Morganthal, age 17*
*May 2014*

# Chapter One

*You Can Change Your World*

# Chapter 1:
## You Can Change Your World

*What made you pick up this book?*

Was it because you are bored during summer break and you have nothing better to do with your time? Was it because your parents bought it for you and so you figured you would give it a chance and see what it is like? Was it maybe because you want to make a difference in your world, only you don't know how?

Well, whatever your reason may be, I don't think that is what matters.

What matters is that you are holding this book in your hands right now.

You see, God planned for you to read this book.

Even now as I sit in my bedroom typing these words before this book is ever even published, I know that God placed these pages in your hands for a reason.

I may not know the names of every person who will read this, but I do know that God does.

He knows you inside and out. He knows your name, your hair color, your eye color, your smile. He knows your favorite things to do and your pet peeves. He knows what excites you and what hurts you. He knows your passions and dreams. He knows the ways that you secretly dream of changing the world around you for the better.

Every time you close your eyes and dare to dream, God smiles.

Because, you see, He wants you to pursue your dreams even more than *you* want to pursue them. He longs to have you join His team and make a difference in the world.

And that leads me to ask you another question...

Have you ever wanted to change the world?

I know that you have. You wouldn't have picked up this book otherwise. But maybe, somewhere along the line, you forgot about that desire to make a difference.

You know the desire I'm talking about.

It is that burning desire deep within all of us to not waste our lives, but to make them count. Maybe that desire first entered your heart when you wondered if there is more to life than iPods and video games. Maybe the desire first entered your heart when you realized that God had so much more for your life than what you had thought was possible.

We don't always notice the desire at first, but it shows up in all of us at some point in time.

But when you do realize the burning desire in your heart to do something with your life, what are you going to do about it?

Some people choose to ignore it and they go on living a normal, comfortable life. Others choose to do something about it... but not right now. They'll do something about it "someday."

And sadly, these people miss out on the great adventure God has planned for each and every one of us. They miss out on the chance to be a part of God at work in the world around them.

Yet there are still those who choose to stand up, shake off the grip of apathy, and use their lives to make a difference for God.

18

Which life do you want to lead?

The choice is entirely up to you. In this day and age, not very many people put high standards on teenagers. They tend to think of them as rebellious and self-absorbed. So if you choose to ignore your desire to change the world and continue to live an unchanged life, no one would probably even question it. They would probably just think of you as a "normal teenager." But in all honesty you really would be settling for less.

You were made for so much more than that.

The reason you have that desire to make a difference is because you were made to change your world. You were created to make a difference. You are alive this day in history for a purpose much greater than yourself. You were not made to live for yourself and your own selfish ambitions. You were made to live your life for Jesus Christ and give it all up for Him.

Sometimes we know this, yet we don't know what it truly means to live for Jesus and make a difference in the world for Him.◆

Well, throughout these pages I would like to invite you to join me on the wild adventure God has planned for us. I can't promise it will be easy, but it will be wonderful.

And now, before I go any further, let me tell you a little bit about myself. I mean, if we are going on an adventure together we should get to know one another a little bit better, right?

I am sixteen years old as I pen these words and I live in the beautiful state of Pennsylvania. I am currently a senior in homeschool high school. I love letters, new books, Dr. Pepper, and caramel ice cream. I also enjoy saying "y'all" even though I'm not southern at all. (By the way, have y'all wondered yet why you picked up this book in the first place?)

I am a normal girl who loves her Jesus with all of her heart. I have decided to accept His invitation to partner with Him in changing the world.

And I hope you will too.

At this point you know more about me than I know about you, but I hope you will still join me on this adventure.

I invite you to stand up, take God's hand, and enter into the special adventure He has planned just for you.

I invite you to ask God what *He* wants you to do to make a difference in the world. A word of caution here: It may not be what *you* want to do.

I invite you to lift your eyes to what is going on around you and ways that you can do something about it.

I invite you to face your fear and not let it keep you down.

You can do this. I believe in you.

But sometimes we all need a little push to actually get off the couch and *do something* about our dreams and our deep desire to change the world.

I pray that this book is your call to action.

I pray that it is the challenge you need to get up and refuse to be silent. I pray this is the challenge you need to take that first step and make your life count for God.

Throughout these pages I am going to talk about God frequently, because *He* is what this is all about. We can't make a difference in the world without Him and we can't truly know what *living* is until we have a relationship with Him.

Maybe some of you reading this don't know all that much about God. Maybe you don't feel like right now you want anything to do with God.

If that is so, *I dare you* to not toss this book out the window right now or let the dog eat it. *I dare you* to keep reading. *I dare you* to take a chance and see what God will do if you open up your heart to Him. Whatever you do, just please don't throw this book away yet. Hang on until the end.

So now, are you ready?

Are you ready to see what God is waiting to do with your life when you give it all to Him? Are you ready to take a risk and do something bigger than yourself?

Then what are you waiting for?

*Let's go.*

*"Therefore He says:*

*'Awake, you who sleep,*
*Arise from the dead,*
*And Christ will give you light.'"*

*~Ephesians 5:14~*

# Chapter Two

*The Lies*

# Chapter 2:
## The Lies

*You're not good enough...*

It has only been a few days since I wrote those words in my personal journal. You see, for a year now I have had writer's block.

And when I say that, I mean I have it *bad*. As far as writing books, well, I haven't done that for a year. In pure frustration I sat on my bed and asked God why I couldn't write. I mean, I had always written well before. I just couldn't understand why everything I wrote I just ended up deleting the very next day.

And that's when God stopped me and showed me the problem.

I didn't think I was good enough. I didn't think I was a good enough writer. I thought that the words I wrote were either boring or, well... not good enough.

I could almost see my Jesus gently smiling down on me and asking, "You aren't good enough in *whose* eyes?"

I sat there for a moment not entirely sure how to respond. Obviously the answer was the world. I didn't think my writing was good enough compared to all the other great authors out there in the world.

That was when God issued a dare to *me*. Yeah, I know, I'm really good at issuing dares but when it comes to accepting them, well, that's a different story.

I knew God wanted me to write for Him. Of course I said that everything I wrote was for His glory alone. But if that were true, then why did I care so much about what others thought of my writing?

The dare I felt God give me was this: *I dare you to write as if you could only ever write one more book. What would you want to share with the world?*

This book is the result of accepting that dare. And, to be honest with you, I still don't feel good enough.

But the truth is that if I waited to feel "good enough," this book would never happen! It is in the moments when we don't feel good enough, but we choose to step out anyway that we realize something important.

*We don't have to be good enough.*

You see, our God is enough! Isn't that a comforting thought? If we allow God to use us, He will make up for our inadequacies and failures.

We just need to stop believing the lies.

And don't tell me you don't know what I mean. We all have lies that we believe. In order to make a difference in the world we must push past these lies and accept the truth that God is offering to us.

So what are some of the lies?

*I'm only a teenager. I'm too young.*

I'm only 16 years old.

Do you think I'm old enough to write a book or make a difference in the world? Well, from the world's standards, I'm probably not old enough. I'm *only a teenager*. But you know what? I know plenty of teenagers who changed their world while they were still young.

God knew that this would be a lie that would silence many young people, so what did He do? He included

26

stories of teenagers in the Bible. Think of Mary, Esther, David, and so many more. These people were just like you and me. They were young and they probably felt very inadequate for the tasks God gave them. But, oh how glad I am that they obeyed Him!

When I am tempted to tell myself that I am too young to really make a difference in the world, I open my Bible to the first chapter of Jeremiah. I then make myself read verses 4-10 until I finally believe them. These words were spoken by God to Jeremiah, but they are also for you and me.

*"Then the Word of the Lord came to me, saying:*

*'Before I formed you in the womb I knew you; before you were born I sanctified you; I ordained you a prophet to the nations.'*

*Then said I: 'Ah, Lord God! Behold, I cannot speak, for I am a youth.'*

*But the Lord said to me: 'Do not say, 'I am a youth.' For you shall go to all to whom I send you, and whatever I command you, you shall speak.*

*Do not be afraid of their faces, for I am with you to deliver you,' says the Lord.*

*Then the Lord put forth His hand and touched my mouth, and the Lord said to me:*

*'Behold, I have put My words in your mouth. See, I have this day set you over the nations and over the kingdoms, to root out and to pull down, to destroy and to throw down, to build and to plant.'"*

*~Jeremiah 1:4-10*

Jeremiah believed the same lie that continues to deceive numerous young people across the world today. *I am only a youth.*

But what did God tell him?

God basically told Jeremiah to not talk like that! *Don't say 'I am only a youth!'*

So why do we continue to believe this lie and use it as our excuse to do nothing during our teenage years?

None of us know how long we will have in this life. We are not guaranteed so many years or days. What if you never got the chance to do something with your life because you thought you were too young, but then time ran out? I think this excuse would seem pretty silly then.

Another verse that throws this lie out the window is 1 Timothy 4:12 —

*"Let no one despise your youth, but be an example to the believers in word, in conduct, in love, in spirit, in faith, in purity."*

Let no one despise your youth. That means, don't listen to those people who tell you that you are too young and that you can't make a difference. But it also means that *you* mustn't despise your youth. You mustn't view your youth as a disadvantage or a hindrance. You need to instead view it as an opportunity to let God do miracles through you.

Please don't believe this lie that you are only a teenager. You are *never* too young to start using your life to bring God glory.


*I'm not worthy.*

Let's be honest.

None of us are worthy.

None of us deserve anything really. We don't deserve the gift of grace and life that God gives to us. But if we deserved it then it wouldn't be grace, would it?

If you want to say you aren't worthy enough to make a difference in this world because maybe you have made mistakes in your past, you need to know something.

We have all made mistakes—mistakes that probably should have disqualified us from making a difference for Jesus.

We broke God's commandments and so we deserve to die and be separated from God forever.

But God sees things differently.

He saw how much He loves us. That's why He sent Jesus. He sent Jesus into this world to give us what we don't deserve. He gave us life and a relationship with Him, even though we aren't worthy of it and we don't deserve it. He gives us grace and gives us second chances over and over.

If we belong to Him, then when God sees us He sees Jesus, and Jesus is more than worthy! So, no, you may never feel worthy of completing the task God has given to you. You may feel like you keep making mistakes over and over that disqualify you from what God has called you to do. But you still need to obey that calling because God has given you enough grace to cover every mistake you have made and every mistake you ever will make. Our dreams and our desire to change the world should all be done for the glory of Jesus Christ, and if that is true, we can know that He is worthy even when we are not.

Not feeling worthy doesn't mean that you don't have *worth*. You have more worth than you know. The reason?

Your worth does not lie in what you have done or what you will do. It is all in Jesus Christ. We don't deserve the gift that God has given us and we may not feel qualified for the task that He has given us. But if you do it with Him, He will make sure that you have all you need.

Let Him work through you.

*I don't have the resources or the ideas I need to make a difference.*

Oh, believe me; I have used this excuse more times than I can count.

I think satan enjoys deceiving us with this lie because it is often the easiest lie to believe.

We can tend to think that if we don't have the resources and ideas we need right in front of us, we should let someone who does have those things make the difference.

I will talk about this more in a future chapter, but I wanted to address it briefly right now, because I bought into this lie for a long time.

I believed that I wasn't smart enough to come up with an idea of ways that I could make a difference in the world. I looked at the ways other people were changing things and I didn't think that my ideas were good enough (there's that lie again!). So I blamed my apathy on the fact that I didn't have the proper resources to do anything.

Really? What was I waiting for? A giant billboard to show up in front of me, telling me what to do and where to do it? Looking back, I wish I could change the years I spent doing nothing about my dreams because I didn't think I had the resources to do so.

What we need to realize is that there will usually never be a giant billboard show up in front of us, telling us what to do. If God wants to do that for you, then sure, He's God. He can do it.

But that usually isn't how He works.

Instead, He usually speaks to us in small ways that are clear signs to us of what He is calling us to do. Even if it looks different from what others are doing.

So stop believing this lie. Instead open your eyes and start looking for where you can get the resources you need. Ask God to dream with you and come up with unique, world-changing ideas together.

*I failed before. I will probably fail again.*

At one point in time I wondered if there was any way I could possibly make any difference in the world when all my ideas seemed to fail.

My dream and my passion are to do something to end human trafficking. There were times when it seemed like my ideas on how to raise money for organizations working to fight slavery in the world just seemed to go wrong.

At one time I decided that I was going to have a benefit concert to raise money and I was going to have a band come and sing. There were plenty of people who warned me that this idea might be a little too ambitious.

However, I have never been one to give up very easily. I also hold the strong belief that with God, *all* things are possible. I told my family that I believed in miracles and I knew that God could pull this off if He wanted to.

Needless to say, the plans for the concert did not work out the way I had intended and I was not able to do it.

At first I was crushed. I felt like I had failed. Not only had I failed to raise money for children in slavery, but I felt that I had also failed God and what He had asked me to do.

For a few months after this I tended to wallow in my self-pity and feelings of failure. But finally I realized something.

*I couldn't give up just because I believed the lie that I had failed and may fail again.*

I began to come up with other ideas that were smaller. Although they wouldn't be as big as a concert, they were more attainable. Sometimes when we fail at something we tend to give up altogether. We don't have the courage to try again. And to be honest with you, it will take sheer courage to risk failing again.

You must be courageous though! You can't give up. You must try again. If you feel you need to, shoot for a smaller goal like I did.

However, I do want to add something. The impossible *can be possible* with Jesus on your side. I still believe that miracles happen. Just because some things seem impossible doesn't mean that they are. Just because your impossible plans failed before, doesn't mean they will again.

When our plans fail we can often think of ourselves as failures. Oh, how many times I thought of myself this way when things didn't turn out the way I thought they should.

But that is also a lie.

You are *not* a failure.

If you only get one thing out of this book, I hope it is that. You are not a failure just because your plans failed.

*"Yet in all these things we are more than conquerors through Him who loved us."*

*~Romans 8:37*

We are not failures. We are conquerors through Jesus Christ!

So get rid of the lie that you have failed and believe the truth about what Jesus says of you.

And then go try, try again.

*If I tried to make a difference, it probably wouldn't even help.*

Sometimes we stop ourselves from making a difference by telling ourselves that we couldn't help anyway. The need is too great, the problem too big, for us to make any difference in the world at all.

Or so we tell ourselves.

This lie can often be the hardest one to push out of our minds. We see the statistics all over the news and Internet, those numbers that are so large they make our minds spin. Before long we become numb to all of the numbers and we feel overwhelmed by how big the problem is in our world.

We all know that there are problems in our world today. Children being sold into slavery, babies being killed, and families going hungry. The list could go on.

When we look at these problems we tell ourselves there is nothing we could possibly do. And even if we did do something, it wouldn't make much of a dent in the enormous problems.

This lie can quickly spread into the lie that, if we can't change it all then why try to change anything?

What happened to changing the world for even just one?

No, we can't change everything that is wrong in the world. We may not even be able to make a dent in the problems.

But if we don't try, what will happen to that one little boy who needs fed, or that one young girl who needs a friend?

When we touch the life of someone else, no matter how small the impact may seem we are truly changing the world. That one person may then go out and touch someone else's life, until eventually the whole world is changed. It creates a ripple effect.

Jesus fed five thousand people with five loaves of bread and two fish, the offering of a small boy. What do you think He would be able to do with your offering, no matter how small?

Jesus is just waiting to do great things through your life, my friend. You only need to step out and choose to let Him use your life, even if you don't think it can make that big of a difference.

And when you do that, trust me, it will be amazing.

What are the lies that are keeping you from all God has for you? Maybe you can identify with some of the lies I shared here, or maybe you are carrying around some lies of your own. Whatever the lies may be that you believe I dare you to stop believing them.

Stand up tall, push aside the lies, and instead believe and accept the truth. Believe the truth that God is whispering to your heart.

What is that truth?

- God wants you to partner with Him in changing the world, just as you are. You don't need to be smarter, look prettier, or act better before He can use you (Isaiah 58:6-8; Acts 9:10-16).
- God wants to do big things through you, especially when you are young (1 Timothy 4:12; Jeremiah 1:4-10).
- You are redeemed, loved, chosen and accepted by God. Stop telling yourself otherwise (John 3:16; Isaiah 41:8-10).
- If you don't have very many ideas or resources available to you and you don't think you can make a difference because of that, think again. God is on your side and if you are doing His will, He will make a way (Romans 8:31-32).
- You are not a failure and you are not a quitter. Don't ever give up (Galatians 6:9)!
- Even the smallest act of kindness or care can change the world for even just one person (Matthew 14:14-20).

- You were created by God to use your life to bring Him glory and praise (Psalm 139:13-18; Revelation 4:11).

No matter how many lies you have believed before, accept the truth now. When you know the truth, it will set you free (John 8:31-32).

And when you are free from the lies, God is smiling and ready to use you… you only need to say yes.

*"Then Jesus said to those Jews who believed Him, 'If you abide in My Word, you are My disciples indeed. And you shall know the truth, and the truth shall make you free.'"*

*~John 8:31-32~*

# Chapter Three

*The Fear*

# Chapter 3:
## The Fear

*Have you ever been so afraid of something that the mere thought of it makes your hands start to shake?*

Well, I have been.

Something you should know about me is that I am *scared to death* of heights. It is so bad to the point that when we are just driving over a mountain I begin to panic. God must have thought it best (or humorous) to have me live in the mountains, so I could get over my fear. Well, we're still working on that.

If we are traveling and I am on the top floor of the hotel, I try my hardest to not get close to the windows. I have never flown in a plane but am certain that I wouldn't be able to handle it.

Something else you should know about me is that I have a fear of bugs. Go ahead and laugh, but it is the truth. My fear of bugs may not be as bad as my fear of heights, but the fear is still there. If there is any kind of bug in the room I am in, I proceed to beg my mom or dad to get rid of it. I am most afraid of grasshoppers, but stinkbugs are a close second (I will never believe my mom when she tells me that as a kid I used to catch grasshoppers).

So why am I telling you this?

I'm telling you this because sometimes our fear keeps us from doing what God has called us to do. What did God call me to do that had to do with my fears you ask?

God told me to go.

To Africa.

Yeah, at first I thought that He might be joking.

He wasn't.

I was almost eleven years old when God shook my world. I was a bubbly, enthusiastic girl who had big plans and dreams for her life. I decided from a very young age that I was going to grow up, get a horse and show jump in the Olympics. It was all I wanted to do with my life. Funny thing was that I had never actually ridden a horse (except at pony rides every now and then. Oh, and you can't forget about my trusty stick horse). That did not deter me however, and neither did my terrible fear of heights. For some reason I managed to forget about my fear when I thought about show jumping on my horse. Maybe it was because I had never actually jumped before.

I was certain that nothing was going to change my dreams and that one day they would come true.

Then one day my family and I went to the annual mission's conference at my church on March 9, 2008.

Truthfully, I don't remember much about the conference that night, but I do remember feeling sad for the children in other countries that the missionaries had been helping. They were homeless, hungry and had no one to take care of them. My heart ached to make it all better.

I could not sleep that night and I watched the clock as the hours ticked by. At one point, I began to pray about the conference and the children out there who had nothing.

At that moment I felt God speak to me in a way I had never felt Him speak to me before. I did not hear an audible voice, but in my heart I felt Him tell me to "go and tell them."

I was young at the time and truthfully I was a little scared. In barely a whisper I asked God where I was to go.

*Africa.*

To say I was shocked is probably an understatement. In that moment I committed my life to God and His will for me, whatever it may be.

Throughout the days and months following that night, I was deeply troubled.

Yes, my heart ached for these children that I had heard about who needed help, but deep inside I wished God had called someone else.

You see, God called me to a small land-locked country in Central Africa…Uganda.

When I was eleven I didn't even know anything about Uganda. If you had asked me to find it on a map, I probably couldn't have. I knew pretty much nothing about this country. All I knew was that it was far, far away. And to get there you have to fly.

*In a plane.*

The mere thought of this made me sick. Oh, and did I mention that Africa also has bugs? Lots of them.

I couldn't help but wonder if God had called the wrong person. Maybe He didn't realize that not only could I not stand to be around bugs, but I also could not fly. I even promised God that I would go wherever He wanted me… just as long as it didn't involve flying.

It wasn't until I was a few months away from turning thirteen that God got a hold of me. He asked me if I was going to be afraid forever and let it keep me from what He had planned for my life.

I gave God everything. I gave Him my fears, my inadequacies, and my dreams. Giving up my dreams may have been the hardest of all, and in all honesty, that was my deepest fear. I was so afraid that if I followed God to Africa, I would have to give up everything *I* had planned for my life.

I did have to give up my plans for my life, but it wasn't as scary or terrible as what I thought. In return for my fears, God gave me faith. In return for my dream of show jumping, God gave me a country that I now love with all of my heart. In return for my brokenness, God gave me beauty.

No, I have not traveled to Uganda yet. I plan on flying (trying not to cringe) to Uganda in a year or so to follow God's calling on my life.

Honestly, I have no idea what awaits me in Uganda.

I have no idea what God has in store.

But I can't wait to see His dream for my life unfold.

His dreams for me were so much more wonderful than my own. They may not be easier, but they are what I was made for.

My dreams kept me comfortable. They kept me safe. They were what *I* wanted to do. They didn't make me face my fears. They didn't take me outside my comfort zone. And while they may not have been the best that God had for me, I was content to stay in my safe little bubble with my safe little dreams.

But God wasn't.

God loved me far too much to let me settle. He loved me far too much to watch me live a comfortable, safe life that didn't mold me into who He wanted me to be.

God had a dream for me that was bigger than I could have imagined. Yes, it did take me out of my comfort

44

zone and in my eyes it wasn't safe. Yes, it wasn't what I wanted to do at first. And, oh yes, it made me face my fears.

But letting God write my story is so worth it.

Trading my dreams for His is worth it.

As a writer, I have always loved stories. I read them, I write them and I tell them. My favorite stories have always been true stories about people who have let God write their life story. If you are a writer (or even if you aren't), you may relate well to what I am about to say.

Imagine for a moment you were writing a mystery novel. You form the characters in your mind. You give them names and describe what they look like. To you they are real. Next you form the plot and the adventures your character must take. In your mind you know how you want it to end and you have a beautiful ending in mind. You decide that your character is going to come upon an old, deserted house. Behind the door is the clue she needs to solve the whole mystery. You know that if she goes in the house, the mystery will be solved and your ending will be perfect.

But what if you couldn't control what your character did? What if your character decided that she was too afraid to walk into that house and so she didn't go in?

After all, at that moment she doesn't know the clue is there. She doesn't know that there is truly nothing to fear behind that door.

However, you as the author know. Wouldn't it be just a little frustrating and maybe disappointing if your character chose not to walk into the house where the clue is? Wouldn't you be disappointed that her fear got in the way of solving the mystery?

Don't you think God sometimes feels the same way?

God knows everything about us. He knows our past, He knows where we are today, and He knows our future.

He created us. With a smile, He named us and made us who we are. He lovingly chose the exact color of our eyes and hair. He set us in the family that was best for us.

And all the while, He had dreams for us. He watched us grow and He was with us every second. He knows how our life stories will end and He knows all the moments in between. And because He loves us, He wants us to experience the dreams He has for us, because truly they are best.

But maybe you are afraid.

Maybe your fear is keeping you from stepping into that house to find the clue that solves the mystery. Maybe your fear is keeping you from pursuing God's dreams for your life because you don't know how everything will turn out.

God does though.

God knows how everything will turn out. He knows whether or not you will follow His dreams for your life, or if you will let fear get in the way.

Whichever path you choose, He will still love you and stand by your side. God doesn't need us for anything, so He will still be able to work out His will. He *wants* to use us though.

But if you let fear keep you down you will miss out on the greatest adventure of your life. The adventure of following Jesus and experiencing His dreams for you.

So what are you afraid of?

Maybe your fear isn't as simple as my fear of heights or as silly as my fear of bugs, or maybe it is.

No matter how small or big your fear is it can be enough to keep you from following Jesus. *If* you let it.

Like I said earlier, my childhood dream was always to own a beautiful horse and show jump in the Olympics. This was all I thought about and dreamed of.

As a little girl, I was horse crazy.

I had been horse crazy for as long as I could remember. My room was being overrun by everything that had to do with horses. Horse pillows and bedspread, stuffed horses, horse books, horse stickers, horse t-shirts, and the list could go on. The only thing that was missing was my very own horse. That was not a problem though, because I was certain that I would get one. I knew *exactly* what she must look like and she *had* to be a Thoroughbred.

My sister and I even turned our living room into a stable at one point in time. We had the stalls for the horses and the jumping courses which were made from shoeboxes. We would then proceed to take our trusty stick horses and "gallop" them down the staircase and "jump" them across our homemade jumps.

I couldn't imagine my love for horses ever going away and I also couldn't imagine giving up my childhood dream.

But God had different plans.

When God called me to Uganda, the thought of giving up my dreams didn't enter my mind at first. Finally though, it began to sink in.

For several months following God's calling on my life, I tried to ignore it. I pushed it to the back of my mind and tried to pretend that maybe I had heard God wrong.

Yet somehow God kept bringing my calling to my thoughts and pulling my heart towards Uganda. He gave

47

me some signs in those months that were undeniable for me. I *knew* He was calling me. But I didn't want to accept it.

In my heart I knew that if, when I was older, I followed God to Africa I would have to give up my dreams. At this point I was still very much horse crazy, so I didn't even want to consider giving up my plans.

But God, who is ever patient with us and so faithful, gently spoke to my heart. I could almost see His smile as He told me that if I could only trust Him, His dreams for my life would be so much better than I could even imagine.

So I did something that was probably the hardest thing I had ever done up until that point. I got down on my knees and through my tears I gave my dreams to God.

"Only please, please give me a love for Uganda that is greater than my love of horses," I prayed with my heart aching.

I won't lie, it wasn't easy. It wasn't until I was about fourteen years old that I finally stopped longing to be able to fulfill the dreams that I had for my life.

God was faithful to answer my prayer though.

It didn't take long for me to realize that my heart was for the people of Uganda. As I read books and researched online more about this beautiful country, I grew to love this place. God gave me a desire to follow Him into Africa and I honestly couldn't imagine doing anything else with my life.

Sometimes when I see a horse, I remember my childhood dreams of show jumping. I remember how much I loved horses, and still do. But I can't help but smile when I realize that while my dreams were good, God's dreams are so much better.

So what is your dream?

Maybe you have a childhood dream that you have been holding onto for so many years. Or maybe you just started dreaming about what you want to do with your life. Or maybe you still don't have any idea of what your dream is.

I don't know your specific dream, but God does. And I can assure you that God placed that dream in your heart for a reason.

Whatever your dream may be, don't forget it. I never forgot my childhood dreams, I just had to learn to let them go and give them to God. He gives us our dreams for a reason. I believe that the reason He gave me mine was so that He could teach me how to let go and trust Him with my life and plans.

God doesn't always change our dreams, but often the thought of this strikes fear in our hearts.

We are afraid that if we talk to God about our dreams, He will ask us to give them up or do something else with our lives. We are afraid that if we give our dreams to God, He will not give them back to us. We are afraid that if He doesn't give them back to us, we will have to live our lives doing something that we don't want to do. We are often afraid that if we follow God's dreams for our lives, He will ask us to go to Africa (Trust me, I know how you feel).

In order to experience all God has planned for our lives and embark upon the adventure *He* has planned for us, we must learn to push past the fear of losing our dreams.

Our life is not our own.

If you are a Christian, you belong to Jesus Christ. Your main goal in life should be to become more like Him and honor Him with your life—even when that means living out His calling on your life.

If God has placed a dream in your heart, then go pursue it. But if at any point He asks you to change your dream, let it go and follow Him.

Whatever your dream may be, you should give it to Him right at the start.

When I gave my childhood dream to Him, He showed me that He had a dream for my life so much bigger than I could have ever imagined. And no, at first, I did not like the idea of going to Africa.

But when we give our dreams to God and begin to live out the dreams He has for us, our heart changes. Before I knew it, I had a deep love for Uganda and the people there. I began to experience the freedom of dreaming *with God*.

Yes, He may ask you to do something completely different than what you wanted to do. Yes, He may ask you to do something that at first glance you really don't want to do. Yes, He may even call you to Africa.

But will you give up your dreams to follow His?

After all, He gave His *life* for you.

So how do you let go of the fear of losing your dreams?

Well, first, you go to God.

Tell Him exactly what you are afraid of. Tell Him your dreams for your life. Share with Him the excitement you have over these dreams and how they are a part of you. Tell Him why you don't want to let go of them. Tell Him everything about how you are feeling. Yes, He already knows it all, but He wants to hear it from you because He loves you. He is longing to listen to you as you pour out your heart to Him.

After you have shared everything with your Heavenly Father, be silent. In your heart ask Him what His dreams are for your life. Then be silent and listen for Him to speak to you. He may speak to you at that moment or He may not. It may take several weeks or years before you know His answer, but He *will answer* you.

And then, dare to dream with God.

Open up your heart to His plans for you and dream with Him. Maybe there is even some way that God can work out for you to be able to pursue both dreams. For example, what if you want to be a doctor but God has called you to go be a foreign missionary? If you dream with God, He could show you how you could be a missionary doctor. God loves to dream with His people, so go dream with Him.

Don't be afraid of letting go of your dreams. Even if your dreams for your life never come true, you must still trust God. You may be surprised at what He gives you in return for your dreams. I guarantee you that His dreams for you are so much better.

And they just might change the world.

### The Fear of Being Alone

Have you ever been afraid of being left all alone?

I want to talk more about this fear in chapter nine, but I thought it would be good to address it briefly here as well. Often we choose to give up on our dreams because we are too afraid of being alone. We are too afraid of being the only one who is passionate about what we are passionate about. We are too afraid of being the only one who dares to make a difference.

We don't want to stand alone. The cost is too risky, isn't it?

I won't lie to you.

If you do what God tells you to do there will be times when you feel like you are all alone.

I have felt those moments as I have pursued God's dreams for my life. When everyone around us leaves, we feel terribly lonely. We begin to wonder if making a difference for Jesus is truly worth it.

But you know what?

*It is.*

Following Jesus Christ is worth it *all*. And when we are truly following Jesus, no matter how many people criticize or walk away from you, you will never be truly alone. We too often forget that Jesus has promised to *never* leave us. He will be standing by our sides no matter what happens. So we are never alone. It may feel that way for a moment, but it isn't the truth.

Fear has a way of blinding us to what is true. When we are so afraid of being the "only one," we lose sight of God and what He has called us to do.

If you want to make a difference for Jesus in this world, it is necessary that you face your fear of being alone. And once you have faced it, push it away and don't dwell on it anymore.

I have felt very lonely in my dreams before. I have felt like I was the only one who cared about the things I cared about. What I didn't realize was that I was wallowing in self-pity (not something I would suggest).

I was *not* the only one and I can almost guarantee that *you* are not the only one either. Yes, it may have been true that not many people around me at that moment shared my passion for ending human trafficking and slavery, or my passion for Uganda. But when I reached out and looked around I realized that there are so many others around the world who share my passion. Ask God to get you connected with others who share your desire to change the world.

You just might be surprised at what He does.

## The Fear of Saying Goodbye

When God first called me to Uganda, some of my first thoughts in the following days were how was I going to say goodbye? I knew that I was too young to pack up and leave for Uganda that year, but even though I had several years until I would actually leave, in my heart I still had a deep fear of having to say goodbye to my family and friends. At first I tried to convince my family to come with me, but I don't blame them for not being thrilled with that idea.

I have always had a close relationship to my family and the mere thought of leaving one day made me begin to panic. I begged God to send someone else because I didn't want to say goodbye to those I loved.

I came to realize that if I gave into my fear of saying goodbye, I would one day miss out on the amazing adventure God had for me. If I let my fear control me, I would not go to Uganda.

To be honest, I still do not want to say goodbye one day. I don't want to have to walk away from my family and get on a plane.

But I have learned to give my fear to God and trust that He will get me through the goodbyes and bring me back again one day.

In Luke 14:26-27, Jesus says—

*"If anyone comes to Me and does not hate his father and mother, wife and children, brothers and sisters, yes, and his own life also, he cannot be My disciple. And whoever does not bear his cross and come after Me cannot be My disciple."*

Before I go any further, I will make something clear. Jesus does not mean that to follow Him you have to literally hate your parents, siblings, etc. What Jesus is saying is that we cannot love them *more than* Him. We have to love Him enough to follow Him, even if it means saying goodbye to those we love.

What has Jesus asked you to say goodbye to in order to follow Him wherever He may lead you?

Has God asked you to follow Him half-way across the world to make a difference in His Name? Has He asked you to move to a different state to do His will there? Has He asked you to change churches or schools to impact more people for Him? Has He asked you to let go of someone you love because the relationship is not what He wants for you?

If you are afraid of following Him because you don't want to say goodbye to family or friends, then let me just encourage you.

Do it anyway.

I dare you to follow Him anyway.

You won't be sorry you did.

Yet there are still times when God doesn't ask us to say goodbye to people in our lives, but the things that control us. Maybe you are afraid that God will ask you to give up a prized possession, a sport, or even personal comfort. You don't want to say goodbye to those things. I know how you feel, but again we can't let this fear control us and keep us from what God has for us.

*"So likewise, whoever of you does not forsake all that he has cannot be My disciple."*

~Luke 14:33

*"So when they had brought their boats to land, they forsook all and followed Him."*

~Luke 5:11

If we are not willing to give up and lose everything for Jesus, then we are not worthy to follow Him. There is no half-way compromise. You can't follow Jesus, but then when things get tough you give up. It doesn't work that way.

We need to be willing to face our fear and say goodbye to those things that God asks us to let go of.

He did it for us.

### The Fear of Trusting God

I have always wondered why it is so hard to trust God.

I mean, our God is good and faithful. He has a good plan and future for us as He tells us in Jeremiah 29:11. He has our best interests at heart always because He loves us more than we could ever comprehend.

So why then do we find it hard to trust Him with everything? Why do we find it hard to trust Him with our future and our dreams? Why do we find it hard to trust Him with our lives?

I think that part of our fear of trusting God has to do with the fact that trusting Him means giving up control. And giving up control of our situation frightens us.

Ever since I was a little girl I have known that Jesus loved me. I was always a strong Christian girl.

But as a thirteen-year-old I struggled with trusting God. I knew that one day He wanted me to follow Him to Uganda, and even though I wanted to, I didn't want to trust Him. I was afraid that if I trusted Him, He would change my plans. Maybe He would call me somewhere else instead. Maybe He would let me get hurt. Fear controlled me and I was so tired of trying to work everything out on my own. I *wanted* to trust God, but I was afraid.

After much reading of the Bible, I realized that God has a lot to say about our fear and trusting Him.

One of my favorite verses was always Proverbs 3:5-6:

*"Trust in the Lord with all your heart, and lean not on your own understanding; In all your ways acknowledge Him, and He shall direct your paths."*

Another favorite verse of mine about fear is Isaiah 41:10—

*"Fear not, for I am with you; Be not dismayed, for I am your God. I will strengthen you, yes, I will help you, I will uphold you with My righteous right hand."*

Trusting God may not be easy, but I can assure you that it is what we were made to do.

We were not made to handle things on our own. We were not made to take care of everything in our own strength or worry about things that we can't change.

No, we were made to trust our lives to the God who made us and knows us better than we know ourselves.

Sometimes He does things that we don't understand, but that doesn't mean He isn't trustworthy. He *always* knows what is best. He has a specific purpose for each one of us on this earth. Everything we go through, even if we don't understand it, is shaping us into the person God wants us to be to fulfill that purpose.

God loves you more than you know.

Would you ever want any harm to come to those you love the most? I'm pretty sure you would agree with me and say that you don't want any harm to come to them.

Well, God has a love for us that is even deeper than the love that we have for those that we love the most.

Trust Him with everything. Yes, it may be scary at first, but you can't go wrong when you are placing your life in the hands of the One who loves you and cares for you. His hands will never let you go, no matter how scary or uncertain your situation may be.

And there is no better or safer place to be.

### The Fear of Fear

Have you ever been afraid of fear?

You know what I'm talking about. It's that fear deep inside of us that fears becoming afraid.

I used to be so afraid of fear that it would make me sick. Whenever I would think about something important that was coming up in my life, whether it would be a test, a speech, or anything of that sort, I would begin to panic. I was afraid that when the time came for those things I would be afraid and would mess up. I was so afraid of being afraid that I didn't realize that in reality I was already being afraid!

Now there are probably some of you reading this that totally get what I am saying, but there are probably others of you who are staring at this page with blank looks on your faces. Don't worry! If you have never been afraid of fear, that is probably a good thing.

Some of us can tend to think that if we are afraid of fear, we will keep ourselves from fearing things. However, what we don't realize is that we already fear something—*fear!*

We can't live our whole lives being afraid of fear because it is keeping us in bondage to fear. It is keeping us afraid.

So how do you stop being afraid?

There isn't an easy answer for this because, honestly, there will come times in your life when you are very much afraid. When you are facing situations which ignite that fire of fear, the question you should ask is not whether or not you are afraid. Rather, the question you should ask is whether or not you are going to press on *in spite of* the fear.

Are you going to let fear control you and stop you from allowing God to use your life to make a difference in this world? Or are you going to stand tall, hold onto Jesus, and keep going anyway?

The choice is entirely up to you.

You may always have fear staring you down. You may always wonder why you are so afraid of doing what

God has asked you to do. You may always want to give up because the fear is too strong.

That is not what matters.

One day when we go home to Jesus and we are standing in His presence, He will not ask us if we were afraid.

He will ask us if we let the fear stop us.

He will want to know if we let the fear keep us from doing His will. He will wonder if we let it keep us from making Him known to this world.

So did you let it keep you down?

If you have let fear control you in the past, you don't have to continue to let it control you today. If you have been afraid in the past, that does not define you in your future.

You are defined by the One who made you.

And He says that you have what it takes, *through Him*.

You can be bold.

You can be courageous.

You can be fearless.

*In Him.*

If you choose to believe this and you give all of your fears to God, He will make you courageous, even when you are still feeling afraid.

Being courageous is not being fearless. Being courageous is staring down your fear and choosing to not allow it to control you.

Which will you choose?

*"But now, thus says the Lord, who created you, O Jacob, and He who formed you, O Israel: 'Fear not, for I have redeemed you; I have called you by your name; you are Mine.'"*

*~Isaiah 43:1~*

# Chapter Four

*The Dare*

# Chapter 4:
## The Dare

*If you have made it this far into the book,* I have a feeling that you truly want to change your world and make a difference for Jesus.

Now you have faced the lies that held you down and kept you captive. You learned the truth and I pray you are firmly standing on it.

You have also stared down the mountains of fear in your life and courageously chose to press on anyway, in spite of the fear.

So what comes next?

What is your next step? What can you do to actually start changing your world and making a difference? What does God want from you now?

Well, I can't give you an exact answer to each of those questions because the answer looks different for each one of us. But throughout the rest of this book I want to issue a dare to you.

A dare to change your world.

Not just any dare though. This is a dare that not only will change the lives of those around you, but it will also change *your* life.

If you choose to accept this dare you will be setting out on your own journey to change your world.

So what is my dare to you?

*I dare you* to know your God.

*I dare you* to trust God's bigger purpose.

*I dare you* to love unconditionally.
*I dare you* to believe in the impossible.
*I dare you* to never back down.
*I dare you* to open your eyes.
*I dare you* to change your world.
*I dare you* to leave a beautiful legacy.

Throughout the next several chapters I will look at each dare in greater detail. Before we begin though, I will let you in on a little secret. I know how you may be feeling right now. This list of dares is quite daunting. It may even seem impossible to you.

But it can be done.

God will stand with you every step of the way and will help you as you dare to do what is impossible without Him.

Oftentimes we prefer to issue a dare, rather than accept one. I love to dare my sister to do things, but whenever she dares me I rarely accept the dare.

We don't always know what the outcome of the dare will be, so it is better to have someone else try it first, before we attempt it.

But that isn't the way this dare works.

Before I began writing these words, God placed in my heart these dares. I figured that, since I was challenging you with them, I should accept them myself.

No, I am in no way perfect in completing the tasks I am daring you to do in this book. And you won't be perfect at them either.

But let's work at them together.

Let's accept the dare together.

Because *together*, we can change the world.

*"For if you remain completely silent at this time, relief and deliverance will arise for the Jews from another place, but you and your father's house will perish. Yet who knows whether you have come to the kingdom for such a time as this?"*

*~Esther 4:14~*

# Chapter Five

*I Dare You to Know Your God...*

# Chapter 5:
## I Dare You to Know Your God

*I have always wondered what it would have been like to be Esther.*

I mean, can't you just imagine it?

Close your eyes and dream with me for a moment. I want you to travel back in time to the Biblical days of Queen Esther.

Imagine being a young orphan, probably in your teenage years. Your whole life you have lived with your father figure, Mordecai. But everything that you thought was perfect was turned upside down in just one, simple moment.

You now find yourself quietly walking through the long corridors and winding hallways of the king's palace. Your gentle footsteps echo off of the tall, marble pillars that surround you. A hushed silence settles over you and the other young maidens with eyes wide, just like yours. You draw in a sharp breath at the beautiful white and purple draperies that hang from the ceiling with golden clasps.

You listen intently as the men who brought you here briefly explain *why* you are here. You strain to hear all the information about Queen Vashti and the search for a new queen.

Your mind begins to spin as you realize that you are going to be here for a very long time. Not only will you

have to go through beauty treatments for a year, but you will also have the possibility of becoming queen.

You, a teenage, normal girl, could be *queen*.

Your heart begins to beat faster at the mere thought of it. And then you begin to wonder if you will ever be "normal" again...

The Bible does not tell us exactly how Esther felt when she was taken to the palace, so this is purely my imagination of what *I* think she might have been feeling. But she was human, so I can only assume that she must have been feeling some fear and uncertainty.

While we are imagining we can't forget about Mary, the mother of our precious Jesus.

Her world too was shaken in just one, simple moment. She also was a young teenager. She was a virgin who was told by a shining angel that she was going to give birth to the Son of God.

Now I don't know about you, but if that were *me*, I would be a little frightened and confused. I would probably have had a lot of questions for that angel!

But, although I can almost see her hands trembling and her eyes growing wide, she does not hesitate. In a sweet, humble voice, she whispers that she will be obedient to whatever God asks of her. I know that God must have smiled at her words, knowing the wonderful, amazing adventure He was about to lead her on.

We can't forget about Jeremiah either.

We talked about him a little bit in chapter two. Like Esther and Mary, he was young and did not believe that he could speak very well much less be a prophet of God.

I can almost hear his heart beating a little bit faster when God spoke to him saying that He ordained him to be a prophet to the nations. I can almost see the anxiety

flashing through his eyes as he hurriedly grasps at the only excuses he has—he cannot speak well because he is young.

God is quick to assure him that these excuses are meaningless. They do not matter to Him. He knew what He was doing when He called Jeremiah and He wasn't going to let him back out just because he was a "youth."

What exactly binds these three young people together?

All three of them, while young, still come from different families, different backgrounds, and different circumstances. They were born in different time eras and different places. Yet their one, simple act of obedience changed the course of history forever. So what exactly do they have in common?

All three of them *knew their God*.

And I don't mean that they knew Him in the sense that they knew *about* Him. They deeply knew God with their hearts, not just their heads.

I really could have used examples of numerous other people in the Bible who did whatever God asked of them—Abraham, Moses, Ruth, Samuel, Rebecca, Abagail, Paul, Timothy, the disciples. But what made all of these people and so many others obey their God?

They really *knew* Him.

You see, knowing God is where your adventure of following Him begins.

You can't truly follow God and give Him your all unless you know Him with your heart.

I mean, sure, you can follow God, claiming that you know Him. But if you don't *truly* know Him, you will more than likely back out when the going gets tough.

And the going *will* get tough. Trust me.

What exactly does it mean to know God with your heart?

Knowing God deeper is a life-long journey that you will be on for the rest of your life. Some people embark on this journey with a lot of enthusiasm, but after a few weeks they lose that fire and begin to stop seeking ways to know Him more deeply and intimately.

Yet there are others who never embark on this journey at all because of the cost it involves. The costs of giving up things that matter to you or letting go of things so that you can know Him better.

If you are one of those people who have never set out on the journey to know God at all, I dare you once again to not throw this book out the window or let the dog eat it. Hang in there and continue to read. If you want to know more information about letting God into your life so that you can begin your adventure of knowing Him, please read *Appendix A* now and join us back here later.

For a long time I was one of those Christians who said that I knew God and I did. But I didn't continue to seek ways to know Him better. Of course I did my devotionals and I read my Bible. I just didn't do it with all of my heart and with a hunger to truly, intimately *know* my God.

For those of you who can relate, you know what I'm talking about. You know how it is when you just "go through the motions," of reading your Bible every day and doing all the other "Christian" things you are supposed to do.

This is what I call *religion*.

But that is not what God wants from us. He longs to have a *relationship* with us. Like two best friends. He wants us to know Him better so that we can love Him better.

What showed me my error? What helped me to realize that I couldn't continue living the way I was living? What ignited a fire in my heart to know God deeper than I had known Him and truly develop a relationship with Him?

I participated in the National Bible Bee.

For those of you who don't know about the Bible Bee, I will explain. I hope that some of you reading this have either done the Bible Bee before or plan on doing it in the future.

The Bible Bee was a big part of my journey to know Jesus more deeply and so I will be talking about it a lot in the coming pages.

But first, let me explain a little bit about the Bible Bee...


### The National Bible Bee[1]

The National Bible Bee was launched in 2009 by the Shelby Kennedy Foundation. Each year thousands of contestants from across the nation will use their summer to study more about God and His Word.

The contestants are divided into three age divisions: primary (7-10), junior (11-14), and senior (15-18). From June 1st to the local contest day in August, the contestants memorize assigned Scripture memory passages, and inductively study a book of the Bible, drawing Greek/Hebrew words and cross-references from it.

On local contest day the contestants will gather at their local host locations and compete. In previous years, there was an oral test where contestants quoted verses.

2014 is the first year that there will be no graded oral test at the local competition.

The contestants also take a written test which consists of 200 questions (for the senior division) and lasts for an hour. The written test is based on our Bible memory verse comprehension and on our knowledge of the Bible book we studied.

The scores from both tests were then added together to determine the overall score of each contestant. Starting in 2014 the written test will be the only scored test.

The top 120 scoring contestants in each age division across the United States then move on to the National competition. They will have additional Scripture passages to memorize and another book of the Bible to study on their own.

At Nationals the contestants will take both an oral and written test. The top 15 in each age category then moves on to a semi-final on-stage elimination round. The top five from semi-finals moves on to the final challenge round.

I first heard about the Bible Bee in 2009.

That year a lot was going on in our lives and I was not able to compete. Looking back, I wish I had chosen to do it anyway.

In 2010 I forgot about the Bible Bee and did not remember it again until January 2011 when I was reading a book that mentioned it.

That year I made the decision to enter into the Bible Bee and compete for the first time. It was a decision that led me on an adventure that changed my life. I have never once regretted my decision to sign up. My Bible Bee journey has been a life-changing one for me.

Since 2011 I have competed every year, making it to the National competition twice by the grace of our faithful God!

I can't really imagine not having the Bible Bee as a part of my life. I look forward to it every year and I am already counting down the days until the 2014 local competition (I guess I'm weird like that, but ask most other Bible Bee contestants and they will probably be counting down too).

For those of you who haven't participated in the Bible Bee, you are probably wondering right about now what this has to do with knowing God deeper. You may even be wondering how the Bible Bee helped to change my life because you may view it as only a competition.

The Bible Bee is *much more* than just a competition.

The Bible Bee is an opportunity to know Jesus more deeply. I don't think this really, truly sunk in for me though until my second year of competing.

I made it to Nationals for the first time in 2011. I had such an amazing time and God taught me so much. The following year, 2012, I competed again. I was in the senior division for the first time.

I believed that I could go to Nationals again since I had made it the previous year. To be perfectly honest, I am ashamed of the fact that I trusted in my own abilities those months. I studied hard, but I did it believing that, *in my own strength,* I could go to the National competition that November.

That year I placed 136th, which did not qualify me in the top National qualifiers.

I wondered where I had gone wrong. I had studied hard. Yes, maybe I could've studied a bit harder, but I really did try. I had done my best at the local contest day.

I didn't understand why God hadn't let me have a high enough score to go to Nationals. After all, I did it for God's glory and to know Him more.

Didn't I?

God placed that question on my heart the day following the release of the National qualifiers. Opening my schoolwork for that day, I saw that the verse of the day was 1 Thessalonians 5:16—

*"Rejoice always."*

I felt like protesting as I read those words, but the gentle words of my ever faithful God whispered to my heart that day.

*"Did you do the Bible Bee for Me?"*

My immediate response was, of course, yes. That day God opened my heart to realize that I had placed too much of an emphasis on making Nationals and I had forgotten why I really did Bible Bee.

Not only had I attempted to do my study and testing in my own strength but I had also acted as though going to Nationals was more important than my actual study time with Jesus.

Of course I didn't think this was true at first. I thought that my motives were to honor God, but my actions spoke differently. I asked God to forgive me and to place within my heart a desire to know Him more. A desire to count everything else as loss compared to being able to know my Jesus more deeply.

That day began my adventure to know Him more.

The day I began my adventure of deepening my relationship with Jesus, He gave me this verse: Philippians 3:8-11. This verse has become very dear to my heart and the anthem of my life.

*"Yet indeed I also count all things loss for the excellence of the knowledge of Christ Jesus my Lord, for whom I have suffered the loss of all things, and count them as rubbish, that I may gain Christ and be found in Him, not having my own righteousness, which is from the law, but that which is through faith in Christ, the righteousness which is from God by faith; that I may know Him and the power of His resurrection, and the fellowship of His sufferings, being conformed to His death, if, by any means, I may attain to the resurrection from the dead."*

Can you confidently say that you count everything else in your life as loss compared to being able to know Him more?

Oh, how many days I prayed and asked God to make *Him* the only desire of my heart!

What exactly does it mean to count everything as loss compared to knowing Him?

How do you desire Him so deeply that He is the only true desire of your heart?

Before we get into this I want to add that knowing God is a lifetime journey. You will never be finished. You will not be able to spend two weeks in study with Him and suddenly think that you know all there is to know about Him. Sorry, that just isn't the way it works. You won't be able to one day just stop learning more about God.

This journey is one that we can't give up on because it determines how we will live the rest of our lives.

If we know God, we will live like we know Him. If we love Him, we will live like we love Him. If we choose Him above everything else, we will live that way.

If you claim religion and you have *head knowledge* of God, you will live your life more for yourself than God. You will live to make yourself happy because you don't truly have a relationship with God. And if you don't truly have a relationship with God you don't really have any reason to change, do you?

To choose God above all else, we must know Him.

Think about your best friend for a moment. You know, it's that girl or guy in your life who you know inside and out. You know him/her so well that you know their favorite ice cream flavor, how they will react in a certain situation, or maybe you can even finish each other's sentences.

Do you remember the first time you and your best friend met though? Did you know everything about them at that time? Did you talk for two hours and suddenly you could finish each other's sentences?

No, of course not! It would be silly to think that you are best friends with someone whom you have only known for a little while. It would be silly to think that you truly *know* them.

To know someone you have to spend time with them. You have to talk to each other and do things together.

It's no different with God.

God can be our best Friend if we will only let Him. If we will only open up our hearts and let Him into our lives.

When I was younger I went through a phase in my life where I was very lonely. I felt as if I did not know anyone who shared my passion for Africa and I complained about it daily to God. I'm sure He just smiled waiting for me to realize the truth.

I might have felt lonely, but I wasn't *alone*.

God is the One who called me to Africa! He knew my heart and He shared my passion. When I finally decided to let Jesus become my best Friend, He was right there waiting for me to come to Him. In those months He truly did become my best Friend.

If I was excited about something, I ran to tell *Him*. If my heart was aching for the people I loved in Uganda, I shared it with *Him*. If I was crying, I rested in *Him*.

And you know what?

God gave me wonderful friends who I can't imagine not having as a part of my life.

If you are feeling lonely, go to God. The first step in knowing Him more is to go to Him and let Him be your best Friend.

But the question remains.

*How* do you know Him more?

*How* do you let Him be your best Friend?

*You say yes.*


### Saying Yes

I breathed deeply of the warm scent of fresh bread baking in the oven. It had been a long day.

I dipped my hands into the warm water and floating soap bubbles as I began to wash another dish.

"Bella, can you come and look at this article for your magazine when you are done? I want to see what you think of it," my sister, Kenzie asked me as she sat at the kitchen table, her blue eyes fixed on my laptop screen.

I sigh and continue to scrub dishes. "Maybe later, Kenzie. I'm busy," I reply with only a hint of frustration. I had been busy working all day and I still had writing projects to finish before the day was over.

"Bella, do you want to come play basketball with me?" a soft voice asks from behind me. I turn to my brother and give another sigh.

With more frustration mounting in my voice, I again say, "No, I'm too busy."

Finishing up the dishes, I retreat to my bedroom and sit down on my bed, pulling out my journal. Next to me, my Bible lays open. With yet another sigh I close the worn, underlined pages and lay it aside.

"Maybe tomorrow," I whisper. "I don't have time right now."

As I work on some letters to my friends, I continue to add more tasks to my mental to-do list.

Ever felt like this?

Ever felt like there were just too many things demanding your attention? School, work, sports, church activities? You get the picture I'm sure.

As I began to head into our music room so that I could give my drum set some much needed practice, I felt God's whisper pulling on my heart.

*"Daughter, do you know Me?"*

"Yes, Lord, of course I'm learning to know You more," I answered half-heartedly as I continued to busy myself with tuning my snare drum.

*"Then why didn't you say yes?"*

I let my tuning key rest on the drumhead and I stopped what I was doing. *Why didn't I say yes?*

Those who know me very well can attest to the fact that I am a—ahem—very fast-paced person (nice way of saying 'hyper'). My mind always seems to be thinking of one hundred things and I very rarely choose to slow down and live in the moment.

I love to check things off of my large to-do list and if I don't get everything done I can feel stressed.

If my family wanted me to join them in playing a game or going on a walk, I usually declined because I was just too busy. I felt like I had to get all of these things done to feel accomplished. I had to be ahead in my schoolwork, write another book, raise money and awareness for slavery, etc. The list could go on.

While none of these things were exactly wrong, they were keeping me from saying yes to what God wanted me to do and they were keeping me from living *this moment, right now.* I was always looking at what was next on my list or what was coming up tomorrow, next week, next year.

But God was asking me to say yes in that moment.

Has God ever asked you to do something really small but you still really didn't want to do it? Exactly how I felt.

"Do I *have* to?" I whined. (Seriously? We actually think we have any right to complain to God?)

*"Say yes."*

The whisper in my heart was undeniable.

I got up from behind my drum set and I took my to-do list and ripped it in half.

The very next thing I did was open my Bible back up and read a few chapters. When I had finished gaining strength from God's words, I whispered back...

*"Yes, Jesus."*

I learned that day that to know Jesus, you have to be willing to say yes to whatever He asks of you. Even if there is nothing in you that wants to do it.

God wants us to know Him by revealing Himself to us as we say yes and do whatever it is He is asking of us.

We learn more about Jesus when we say yes and go play that game with our siblings. Even if your siblings drive you crazy (and sometimes they can, trust me), if you say yes to God, I can almost guarantee that you will have fun. And what will God reveal to you? He will show you the beauty of life in your sister's eyes or brother's laugh. He will show you the beauty that He created and you will learn a little bit more about His character and how much He loves you.

We learn more about Jesus when we say yes and go shine God's light into those darkest places. What will God reveal to you? He will meet you in those places and you will see the power of His strength and love.

We learn more about Jesus when we say yes and believe that our God is a miracle-working God, even when situations seem impossible. What then will God reveal to you? He will show you His faithfulness and grace that makes anything possible.

You learn more about God by saying yes.

You learn more about Him by going where He says to go, serving how He says to serve, loving who He says to love, and changing what He says to change.

You learn more about Him by partnering with Him to change your world.

So what did I do that day when God asked me to say yes?

I tossed out my lists and I decided to find God in the simple, beautiful moments of life where He reveals Himself to us and invites us to know Him more.

I walked back into my kitchen and sat down next to my sister. "Kenzie, can I see your article?" And I read it.

Then I went and I played basketball in the driveway with my brother, listening to the birds sing songs to their Maker.

Every moment that I took time to slow down and learn more about God in the simple moments, I realized that I was learning to know Him more deeply.

*Yes, Jesus…*

What is your yes? What is it that God is asking you to say yes to right now?

Go do it.

I guarantee that you will be amazed at how God draws you closer to know Him more.


*Spending Time with Him*


Like I said earlier, you can't know your best friend better if you don't spend time with them, getting to know them.

You might be protesting right now. You may be thinking, "Sure, but that's easy with your friends. You can hang out with them and go to the mall and dinner. How do you do that with God?"

You do it the same way you do it with your friends.

83

God is always right there. He will never leave us. He will never forsake us (Hebrews 13:5).

When you go to the mall, He is right there. When you go to dinner, He is right there. When you are alone in your room, He is right there.

It's like your cell phone.

Okay, don't say anything yet until I'm done explaining. Some people use wind as an example to explain how God is always with us.

I chose to use cell phones.

When you send a text message to a friend or you call a friend, you can't see the radio waves in the air that send that message or make that call. But you know they are there. You know they are there because you see what they are doing.

God's the same way.

We may not be able to physically see Him, but we know He is there. We see the beauty of the world He created all around us. We see the people He made in His image. We see Him working in our lives to do things that we never thought possible.

Make your heart aware of the fact that nothing you do goes unseen by God. Make your heart aware of the fact that He is right there with you. If you want to know Him more, look around you. See Him in the people and things that He created with a smile on His face and love in His heart.

Choose to spend time with your God the way you would choose to spend time with your friends.

Have a conversation with God by praying and listening. Read more about Him by studying His Word. Do things with Him by loving the people He has put in your life.

The ways to spend time with God are really endless.

## Prayer

Ever since I began writing as a little girl, I have loved words. Words were always special to me. Words were how I communicated with others and expressed my thoughts. So maybe I can tend to talk a little too much and a little too fast, but I really am working on that.

When I was fourteen-years-old I had family and friends sponsor me to be completely silent for 25 hours to raise money and awareness for an organization helping child soldiers in Central Africa. At first I thought this would be easy and I was looking forward to it.

About 3 hours into it I thought quite differently.

I think it is safe to say that I was miserable. I was very frustrated that I could not communicate to my family about *anything*. Some of my family said that they enjoyed the silence (their names are omitted to protect the guilty). The only reason I kept going was because I was doing it for a cause I truly believed in.

Why am I telling you this?

Because words are how we communicate with each other. The words could be written or spoken or even signed. But either way we all use words every day to communicate.

Try going without speaking for a day and you will quickly see my point that it is impossible to have a relationship with someone if you are not able to communicate. And if you decide to go silent for a little while, sign language is not allowed either as my sister had to remind me.

If you can't have a relationship with someone without communicating with them, what do you think we need to be doing with God?

That's right! You need to talk to Him (you're catching on pretty quickly).

Our communication with God is called prayer.

I'm sure you know what prayer is. Most of us have either heard other people pray or we pray before meals and bedtime. While that is great, that is not exactly what develops a deeper relationship with God.

When I set out on my journey to know Jesus more deeply, I dared myself to not allow prayer to be a routine in my life that was just another thing I could check off my to-do list. I wanted to be able to go to God in prayer as easily as I breathed.

I decided that I wasn't going to pray just during meals, before going to sleep, or when I needed something.

I have noticed that a lot of people—even Christians— tend to only go to God in prayer when they need something.

Well, I have news for you; God is not a vending-machine.

When do you talk to your best friend?

Do you call them up only when you need something from them? Well, if you are anything like me your answer would be most certainly not! You call your best friend when you have exciting news, are hurting, or even when you just feel like talking about anything and everything.

Why is it different with God?

I did not want my relationship with God to be something that I invested in only when I needed help with something. And I dare you to not allow yours to be that way either.

Talk with God about anything, the way you would with your best friends. Praise Him and worship Him by giving Him the glory for what He has done and is doing in your life. Thank Him for the blessings He has given you. Tell Him where you have gone wrong and ask Him to forgive you.

Yes, God knows everything about your life. He knows your thoughts, your failures, and your dreams. But that doesn't mean that He doesn't want to hear it from you. Because He does.

We also need to remember though that communication is a two-way street.

When we talk to our friends we also take time to be silent and listen to them share about their day and the things going on in their lives.

If you want to truly know Jesus deeper, you have to listen to Him and what He is saying to you. Take time to be still and listen for His voice.

Oh, and the good news?

If you ever decide to go silent for several hours, you will still be able to communicate with Jesus even if you can't talk to anyone else.

He knows our thoughts and hearts so we can talk to Him without even saying anything out loud. That's the beauty of it. You can talk to Him anytime, anywhere…even without using words out loud.

So we know that in order to know God deeper we must talk to Him and also listen to Him talk to us. But sometimes God doesn't choose to audibly speak to us and tell us what He wants us to do.

Sometimes God doesn't use billboards. What do you do then?

You read your Bible and you study it.

The Bible is God's Word to us and it is the things that He wanted us to know. When we read the Bible we learn more about God by seeing Him revealed through history. We see His attributes and learn more about Him that way.

But when we read our Bible we can also hear God speaking to us. He sometimes chooses to reveal His will for us through His written Word.

And when I say Bible study, I do not mean for you to pick up your Bible, read a chapter, and then put it back on the shelf to gather dust bunnies.

For those of you reading this who have participated in the Bible Bee, you know what I mean by Bible *study*.

The Bible Bee was such an amazing tool God used in my life to not only bring me closer to Him, but also to help teach me what true Bible study is.

Before participating in the Bible Bee I considered my Bible study the times that I would read a few chapters in the Bible and pray a quick prayer, asking God what He wanted to teach me. However, there were times when my mind would wander during my reading and I could probably not tell you much about what I read. Ever done something like that?

Let me clarify something quickly. Reading your Bible is great. If you read a few chapters, that is wonderful. My point is that if you want to develop a closer relationship with Jesus and know Him more deeply, you need to do more than *just* that.

When I began competing in the Bible Bee, I began to use Greek lexicons, commentaries, and Bible concordances. I also suggest keeping a journal of Bible verses that are important to you, things you are learning about God, and what God is teaching you. Maybe you could call it your, "Knowing God" journal or some other cool name that I can't think of at the moment. Come up with your own ideas (they will probably be better than mine anyway).

Concordances and Greek dictionaries are a big help as well. If God is leading you to a certain passage or topic, these tools can help you get more out of it.

Let me give you a quick example.

Maybe you want to learn more about the attributes of God so that you can know more about His character. You could take just one attribute—like His love—and go from there. Using a Bible concordance or topical Bible you could look up verses that have to do with God's love. After you have your verse, look up the word *love* in a Greek dictionary and search for the meaning that is being used in the passage you are studying.

Now if you have never done this sort of thing before you may be thinking that this seems like a lot of work.

It may seem that way at first, but I can guarantee you that once you begin studying God's Word more intensely, you will be amazed at how much fun you have with it. It is truly a special, awesome way to spend time getting to know God more deeply.

Trust me; you will never regret the hours spent in study of the Bible.

Those hours will be the ones to sustain you in the hard times.

They will be the ones that help you know your God more deeply and give you direction on how God wants you to change your world.

### Scripture Memorization

*"With my whole heart I have sought You; Oh, let me not wander from Your commandments! Your Word I have hidden in my heart, that I might not sin against You. Blessed are You, O Lord! Teach me Your statutes. With my lips I have declared all the judgments of Your mouth. I have rejoiced in the way of Your testimonies, as much as in all riches. I will meditate on Your precepts, and contemplate Your ways. I will delight myself in Your statutes; I will not forget Your Word."*

*~Psalm 119:10-16*

The 119th chapter of Psalms has always been one of my favorite chapters in the whole Bible, because it is all about God's Word.

I could have really written out the entire chapter here, but I chose to only give you some of my favorite verses from the chapter. Maybe you could read the whole chapter on your own.

I have always been passionate about Scripture memorization, and the Bible Bee really helped to deepen that.

Have you done much Scripture memorization lately?

Studying our Bibles is great, but another vital part of that is memorizing them.

I also want to add that anyone can memorize Scripture. God has placed this ability in each and every one of us. I believe that with all of my heart.

God would not have placed the instruction in the Bible to memorize Scripture if He did not give us the ability to do so.

Read the verses from Psalm 119 again.

God wants us to seek Him with our whole hearts by studying and memorizing His Words.

I mean, think about it. The Bible is God's *love letter* to us! If someone you loved sent you a love note, or even if a good friend just sent you a letter, wouldn't you read it and then re-read it again? This letter would be special to you and, if you are anything like me, you will read it over and over again.

Why do we treat God's Word differently?

When we view the Bible as God's special love letter written for *us*, we will treat it differently. Suddenly it becomes new to us and we want to keep reading it and getting more out of it. We want to memorize it so that our True Lover's words are never far from our hearts or minds.

During Bible Bee season, I memorize a lot of verses. Last year, because I was a National qualifier, I had a total of about 800 required memory verses. I also memorized on my own about 400 or so extra verses. This brought my total to around 1,200 verses in six months.

Listen to me while I say that this was *only* by the grace and faithfulness of God. I could never have done that on my own.

I am not saying that you have to memorize over 1,000 verses in the next six months. If you are in the Bible Bee then maybe you will want to. My point in telling you that was to make you realize that God gives us the strength to memorize Scripture.

Even though I memorize so much during Bible Bee, I also like to keep up with memorization when Bible Bee is over for the year. Of course I don't memorize as much, but I like to make sure that I try to do at least a passage a week.

If you are just beginning to memorize, I suggest that you begin with a small verse or two. Maybe choose your favorite passage. Once you have it memorized, continue to think about it throughout the day and what it means to you. This is called meditation. By the end of the day, I'm pretty sure that you'll be able to quote it by heart. Although keep in mind that you can't *just* memorize Scripture. You also must live it out.

Hide God's Word in your heart and live it out, dear readers.

Then you can confidently say with the Psalmist that, *"I will delight myself in Your statutes; I will not forget Your Word!"*

*"One thing I have desired of the Lord, that will I seek: That I may dwell in the house of the Lord all the days of my life, to behold the beauty of the Lord, and to inquire in His temple."*

*~Psalm 27:4~*

# Chapter Six

*I Dare You to Trust God's Bigger Purpose…*

# Chapter 6:
## I Dare You to Trust God's Bigger Purpose

*I stared at the tall building in front of me,* my heart pounding loudly in my ears and my throat completely dry. Tears burned my eyes but I refused to let them slip down my cheeks.

The day was October 8, 2013 and it was 8:49am.

The streets of Maryland were crowded and I clung to my sister's arm tightly. Staring at the hospital in front of me seemed to take my breath away as my pulse quickened again.

With all of my heart I wished that I could fast forward time and be done with this. I wished that I could take the pain and fear away from my sister. I wished that I could protect her.

But I couldn't.

You see, my twin sister, Kenzie, was having surgery that day.

A surgery that I could not take away from her. A surgery that I could not stop. I felt sick at the mere thought of it.

This story is one that is best shared from her perspective and she has been gracious enough to allow me to include her article, *Keep Me Broken,* in this chapter. I will briefly explain the surgery though.

How many of you fear going to the dentist?

Well, my sister has always had a fear of dentists so it seemed entirely unfair to me that she would have to go through oral surgery.

An X-ray revealed that Kenzie's upper left wisdom tooth was missing. However, upon further examination they realized that it was not missing, but instead up underneath her eye.

If you have ever wished that you aren't so different, just be glad that you aren't *this* unique. In the words of my amazing sister, "Some teenagers have iPods or iPhones, but I have an 'eye tooth!'"

Kenzie's oral surgeon confirmed that it was a cyst that had pushed the tooth under her eye. A biopsy and a couple X-rays later, she had a drain in the back of her gum, trying to drain out the cyst.

Yes, it was gross.

Surgery was basically the only option to remove the cyst and the tooth. If left alone, the cyst could possible push the tooth into her eye or brain.

I remember feeling completely confused, angry, and frightened after we scheduled surgery for September 23, 2013.

When September rolled around, Kenzie caught a cold. We all began to panic and pray fervently that it would just go away. She was not allowed to have any cold symptoms within two weeks of surgery.

Yet the cold lingered.

Surgery was canceled.

I stood in our kitchen and watched as my sister cried and wondered why this had to happen.

I had my own questions too.

I wanted to know why her surgery had to be canceled. I wanted to know why she had to endure this pain every day, because, yes, it was very painful. I wanted to know why she had to go through this at all.

My sister is the sweetest person you will ever know and I love her very much. She is my encourager, best friend, and dare-to-do-anything girl. I didn't think she deserved this at all and I asked God why this had to happen to *her*.

It would not be until after her surgery that God would show me something important.

You see, my sister was in the middle of a miracle.

Only a year and a half prior I had held my sister's hand while she expressed to me her dreams of making a difference in the world.

"I want to do something with my life," she confided. "I want to see God make a miracle happen through me. Only, I don't know what that looks like."

And from that night on, I prayed every night for God to make that miracle happen.

And He did.

It just wasn't in the way that we wanted.

But sometimes I think that the best miracles are the ones that we don't plan. The best miracles are the ones when God turns ashes into beauty, pain into healing.

The best miracles are the ones that only God could orchestrate.

Weeks before surgery, my sister wrote an article that we would all later see as part of her miracle.

Even through the fear and pain, she turned to God. Without knowing what the future held, she clung to God and *chose* to trust Him.

And her miracle came just in time.

# Keep Me Broken
## By: MacKenzie Morganthal

In October of 2012, I went in to the dentist office to get a routine X-ray done.

My dentist was just checking to see where all of my wisdom teeth were. After the X-ray was taken, my dentist sat down with us and explained the picture. He showed my parents and I where three of my wisdom teeth were and then explained that my upper left wisdom tooth was missing. A month later, in November, I went in to the dentist again because I was having some pain and swelling in my upper left gum tissue in the back of my mouth. This time I went in to my Mom's dentist and he reviewed my panorex X-ray that was taken in October.

He was shocked when he saw the X-ray and showed us where my 'missing' wisdom tooth was. My upper left wisdom tooth was up near my eye socket. I was surprised; it was just so weird. I like to be unique, but not *that* unique! ☺

Our dentist referred us to some local oral surgeons, but none of them had ever seen anything like this before. They all said that they could perform surgery to remove the tooth, but we did not feel comfortable with that since they didn't really know about this kind of situation. My parents went back to our dentist and asked him if he could refer us to any specialists who may have seen this kind of thing before.

Our dentist told us about a specialist, a Pediatric Oral Surgeon, about two hours from our home. My parents read his biography online and were impressed with his credentials and experience and wanted to meet with him.

My mom called the office right away to make an appointment but we had to wait about 4 weeks until we could get in to see him. Until that appointment, all we could do was keep guessing—wondering why my tooth was up near my eye socket.

I was very confused at why all this was happening. I remember since the time I had heard the news about the tooth, I sent up many desperate prayers. My Mom had found on the internet some stories of people who had experienced the same thing and had found out that there was a large cyst that had pushed their wisdom teeth into odd places. I began to worry that maybe that's what had happened to my wisdom tooth. I knew that if this was the case, I would need surgery, and that was the last thing I wanted to do. I was scared to death of the idea of getting surgery.

So I began to pray for healing.

I prayed harder and believed more than I ever had before. I asked God for complete healing and pleaded for the tooth to just disappear. I knew that on April 9th I would have a dental CAT scan done that would show in 3D picture where my tooth was exactly and what had pushed it up there or if it had just grown there. I was so worried about that CAT scan and prayed that when we had the scan taken, the tooth would just be gone and not even be there.

When I had first begun to pray for healing, I found myself not really believing that my prayers would come true. But a few weeks before my appointment with the specialist, I truly began to believe what I was praying. I was so confident in the fact that God would give me my miracle and completely heal me. I had even promised God that I would share my story with everyone and tell everyone I knew about how God had given me a miracle. I didn't even fear surgery anymore because I knew that God would heal me.

On April 9th I walked into the doctors' office and had that dental CAT scan taken. I could barely wait to see that scan on the computer and have proof of how God had healed me.

I remember the doctor walking into the room and bringing up the scan on the computer all the while my heart was pounding in excitement. But when the scan appeared and I saw my wisdom tooth still positioned up near my eye socket, my heart just dropped. It was a feeling like none other. I felt like crying as I stared at that computer screen. I felt abandoned. My heart was crying out to God.

Had He not heard my prayers? Did He not care? Why had He forsaken me? In that moment I felt more alone than I ever had before.

The doctor showed us the lining of a cyst that had formed around my wisdom tooth and had pushed it up that far. He told me that normally, people have about 10 to 12% of hollow space in their sinus cavity, but because of the cyst, I had only about 1% or less. He also told me that I would need a biopsy on the cyst to see what kind of cyst it is and if it is cancerous or not. I started to panic when he told me that he could perform the biopsy in about an hour. I had not come prepared to have a biopsy done!

My Mom and I walked out into the hallway of the building and I started to cry. I couldn't stop the tears and my Mom just held me. I told her that I thought God would heal me...I had prayed and believed. She said that God chose to heal me in a different way than what I had wanted, but that everything would work out just fine. I had trouble believing that.

I was very afraid as I went in for that biopsy. It was a very traumatic experience being fully awake for it. I didn't experience much pain because I was numbed, but I felt a lot of pressure and scraping and was very terrified.

After the biopsy was done, the doctor explained to me that he had put a drain in the gum tissue in the back of my mouth. He said that the drain would help to shrink the cyst by draining the material of the cyst out of it. He told us that the smaller the cyst was, the less likely the chance of reoccurrence would be after surgery.

Then the doctor gave my parents a syringe and a prescription for oral medicine and told them that they would have to use the syringe to irrigate my drain twice a day with the medicine. He also said that we would have to do this for the next 6-8 months. I was shocked and hoped he had really meant to say weeks instead of months. He explained that after the drain had been in for 6-8 months then he would do surgery to remove the cyst completely as well as the tooth.

I left that doctor's office that day in pain physically and emotionally. I thought for sure that if God would make me go through surgery that He would have it be within the next couple weeks so that I could have it over with quickly. And then I was told that this would be a long process. I was scared. It was like my prayers had backfired on me.

For the first week after my biopsy my parents couldn't irrigate my drain because I was in so much pain and swelling from the biopsy. But when they were finally able to irrigate the drain, I realized how painful the

103

irrigating process would be for the next 6-8 months. And to make matters worse, I could taste the material draining from my cyst and it was a constant reminder of the valley I was walking through.

About a week after the biopsy, we went back to the office for the results of the biopsy. The doctor told us that the cyst is not malignant. It is benign (Not cancerous. Yay!). He did say though that the cyst is very aggressive. It is called an Odontogenic Keratocyst Tumor because the cyst acts very much like a tumor.

For the next several days, I was thankful that the cyst was not cancerous, but I couldn't get over the hurt that I felt after not getting my miracle. I refused to let my hurt go and slowly found that I was growing angry with God. Why was He doing this to me? He knew how scared I was. Maybe He just didn't care. In that time I could barely even pray. I was so angry and hurt and found myself not even reading my Bible. It was a very dark time for me and I felt that even if I did pray, God wouldn't hear me.

Finally, I decided to open my Bible. The verses I read brought me to my knees in tears.

2 Corinthians 4:7-9, *"But we have this treasure in earthen vessels, that the excellence of the power may be of God and not of us. We are hard-pressed on every side, yet not crushed; we are perplexed, but not in despair; persecuted, but not forsaken; struck down, but not destroyed."*

2 Corinthians 12:8-10, *"Concerning this thing I pleaded with the Lord three times that it might depart from me. And He said to me, 'My grace is sufficient for you, for My strength is made perfect in weakness.' Therefore most gladly I will rather boast in my infirmities, that the power of Christ may rest upon me. Therefore I take pleasure in infirmities, in*

*reproaches, in needs, in persecutions, in distresses, for Christ's sake. For when I am weak, then I am strong."*

Isaiah 43:1-2, *"But now, thus says the Lord, who created you, O Jacob, and He who formed you, O Israel: 'Fear not, for I have redeemed you; I have called you by your name; you are Mine. When you pass through the waters, I will be with you; and through the rivers, they shall not overflow you. When you walk through the fire, you shall not be burned, nor shall the flame scorch you."*

Those verses made such an impact on me and changed my whole thinking process. Suddenly I could see that I was not alone. I could feel God's presence with me and His peace filled my heart. I still did not know God's reasons for having me go through this journey, but I was content in the fact that He has a great purpose for it all. His grace is sufficient for me.

My faith and hope were put to the test a couple weeks later when in the middle of May my drain began to come out. I was terrified and wondering what was happening. I was tempted to question God again, but instead I told Him that I would trust Him. The drain went back into place but the following day it disappeared and completely went up into my cyst. We once again went to see the specialist and he took another X-ray and confirmed that the drain had indeed gone up into my cyst. He instructed my parents to keep irrigating the hole where the drain was supposed to be and told us that he would probably do surgery a bit sooner since we were having problems with the drain. He scheduled us an appointment with him on July 18, 2013 to take another X-ray and to plan surgery.

In the days that followed, there were times when I would get worn down by the task of irrigating the hole

and the pain that it would cause. I began to doubt God's plan again, but would always stop myself. In those days, I discovered what true praise was. As I began to praise God in my darkest moments, my perspective would change. I realized that this journey is not about me. It's about God and what He can accomplish through this. When we can learn to praise and glorify God in our darkest times, I think that is when He can use our stories so much more.

On July 18, I had another X-ray taken and found that my cyst had shrunk quite a bit and my tooth even came down a little bit! All I can say is 'praise God'! We have scheduled my surgery for September 23, 2013. As I heard about the surgery and what all would happen, I began to get scared. But I still have a peace inside. I don't know what next month will bring, but I know that I am going to choose to trust God and praise Him through this storm.

A couple months ago, my prayers were all about what God could do to make me feel better and more comfortable. But I'm learning to pray differently now. My prayer has now become 'keep me broken, God. If that's the way You will be most glorified, then keep me broken.'

I have learned a lot about praise and glorifying God through this journey. It doesn't matter what I'm going through, God stays the same and will never change. I can choose to praise His name no matter what I'm going through, because He doesn't change in the midst of a hard journey. There is a song that says, 'Bless the Lord, O my soul.' As I've walked through these past couple months, that song has become my prayer. As I praise

Him in the midst of this, I pray that it brings so much glory to His holy name.

Soli Deo Gloria — *to God alone be the glory!*

*~~MacKenzie Morganthal*
*(August 2013)*

My sister learned a lot through the whole experience of her surgery and so did I.

While God always has a perfect plan, sometimes that plan is different than the plan that we have for our lives.

Sometimes His miracles are different than what we want.

Kenzie bravely faced her surgery, trusting that God would hold her through it all. She trusted that God knew the bigger picture and that He wanted what was best for her, even if that meant keeping her broken so that He could mold her into who He wanted her to be.

Kenzie's article was published in my monthly e-magazine as well as two other Christian girl magazines. The response she received from the article was unbelievable.

People wrote to her from all over the country, people she didn't even know! They shared how God had used her story to touch them. Many times the sweet letters would bring all of us to tears.

One day Kenzie looked up and, with tears in her eyes, whispered, "God gave me my miracle. I hated that I had to go through this, but this is my miracle. God always makes beauty from ashes."

How true that is.

I'm not sure what you are going through today, but God does.

Maybe your parents are divorcing, your dad lost his job, or a close family member died. Maybe you just feel lost and alone.

Have you ever wondered if God really knows what He is doing?

Have you ever felt so hurt that it seems like nothing good could come out of your situation? Have you ever wished that your life could just be perfect?

Well, God doesn't usually use perfect.

God usually doesn't use perfect, because if He used perfect *His* power, mercy, and grace would not shine through. He uses the weak and the inferior to display His power and His might.

He truly does make beauty from ashes.

Whatever trial you may be going through, my heart aches for you. I wish that you didn't have to go through all the pain and heartache. I wish that things could suddenly get better.

But if you were spared from all of that, God could not use you in the same way.

Kenzie had to go through lots of pain and hurt, but God turned the situation into something beautiful.

He turned it into a miracle.

I will never forget the day that I walked into the hospital with my sister, waiting for her surgery.

I broke down and began sobbing three times throughout that day (Yeah, I counted). I felt weak and very untrusting.

When they gave Kenzie the "happy juice" to calm her down and make her loopy, I began to panic, knowing that they would take her to the operating room soon. Oh,

and for those of you who are wondering: no, she did not act loopy on the medicine so we sadly have no funny stories to share with you (so maybe we have one, but you'll have to ask her about that).

It was not until they began to take her to the operating room that I realized just how untrusting I was being.

I did not want to trust my sister to God.

Have you ever felt that way?

I mean, we know that God loves us and that He always knows what is best. But we also know that sometimes *best* is not always what *we want*.

I was so afraid that something would go wrong during this fragile surgery, and I did not want to trust God with it because I was even more afraid that He would let things turn out differently than how I wanted them to turn out.

That day I chose to trust God.

Even though I was afraid, I gave my sister and the surgery to Him.

I told Him that no matter what happened, I would trust Him.

No, it was *not* easy.

But I did it anyway.

And so can you.

Whatever it is that you are going through, give it all to God. Place it in His hands, stop worrying about it, and just trust.

No, things may not turn out in the exact way that you want them to turn out. According to your plan, things may seem to go terribly wrong.

But are you willing to believe that God knows the bigger purpose and that He loves you always?

*God loves you.*

He hurts for you when you are hurting and He longs to hold you through the pain.

I can't promise that things will get better right away. I can't even promise that things will ever go back to normal.

But what I can promise you is that my God never changes.

My God is faithful.

My God is trustworthy.

My God is always there.

My God wants what is best for me.

My God knows the bigger picture.

*My God loves me.*

Go ahead and think of some attributes of God on your own. Think of the attributes that mean the most to you — His love, faithfulness, mercy, grace, or whatever else it may be. And then believe that, no matter what happens in your life, these things that you know about God will *never* change, because *He* never changes.

Trust God's perfect plan for your life. Yes, it is hard.

Oh, believe me; I *know* it's hard.

Trust Him anyway.

Even if nothing seems to change in your life and things only seem to get worse, keep trusting Him.

*I dare you to trust Him.*

Eventually I'm pretty sure that your perspective on the situation will change and you will begin to see treasures that you never saw before.

*"I will give you the treasures of darkness and hidden riches of secret places. That you may know that I, the Lord, who call you by your name, am the God of Israel."*

*~Isaiah 45:3~*

The treasures of darkness.

Riches stored in secret places.

What are the treasures and riches in your dark situation?

I know that they are there because God promised them.

During Kenzie's long journey, it was hard at times to find our treasures of darkness. At times we wondered if the riches were stored in a secret place that we just couldn't find.

But we realized that the treasures of darkness were right in front of our eyes the whole time. Not only did Kenzie's story impact so many lives, she was also able to meet many wonderful friends and be an example to so many.

The treasures are there in the darkness if you only dare to search them out and find them.

The miracles are waiting right around the corner. The riches sometimes aren't even in secret places at all, but are right in front of your eyes.

You only need to open your eyes to see them.

I know that sometimes in life the storms and the rain don't seem to stop and they can blur your vision.

It is as if you are stuck in a hurricane that just keeps knocking you down over and over again. The rain is insult to injury.

But in the times when the rain won't seem to stop, we just need to trust in God and know that, even when we are standing in the middle of wondering why, He knows *exactly* what He's doing. He sees the bigger purpose, even when we can't, because He is the One writing our life story.

Right now as I write this, rain is pouring down outside my window. Tiny water droplets send streaks down the window as I stare out at the bleak scenery.

And as I watch the rain, Jesus gently whispers to my soul.

You see, without the rain there wouldn't be rainbows. Without the storms there wouldn't be puddles to dance in. And without the rain, flowers wouldn't bloom into beautiful colors.

So it is with our lives.

Without the trials we wouldn't grow stronger. Without the testing we wouldn't be refined. Without the difficult times, we wouldn't have the chance to feel the arms of Jesus wrap around us, and remind us of what we know.

When you decide to change your world for Jesus Christ, the storms will come. I will promise you that.

People, circumstances, heartache will threaten to stop you and put out the fire of your dreams.

This is when it is most crucial to learn to trust that God knows the bigger purpose and *choose* to press on anyway.

Even when you are standing there in the rain, screaming at the dark sky and begging God to just tell you why, remember to look up and hold on to what you know about our God.

When the storms of life come your way, face them with Jesus and trust that He will pull you through.

And then, my friends... *go dance in the rain.*

*"Trust in the Lord with all your heart, and lean not on your own understanding; In all your ways acknowledge Him, and He shall direct your paths."*

*~Proverbs 3:5-6~*

# Chapter Seven

*I Dare You to Love Unconditionally...*

# Chapter 7:
## I Dare You to Love Unconditionally

*Love.*

What comes to your mind when you hear this little, four-letter-word?

When I hear this word, lots of thoughts come to my mind. I think of that warm feeling in the pit of your stomach that makes your heart skip a beat. I think of my family and friends who mean so much to me. I think of some of my favorite things, like hot summer days, pizza, and whipped cream. (I've never tried eating them together, but that's a thought...)

But more importantly, I think of nail-pierced skin and a cross on a hill. I think of love that was shown in action, a love that was so unconditional that not even death could stop it. And I think of the pain that sometimes goes along with loving others.

You see, love isn't a feeling.

Yes, sometimes when you love someone or something, you have that gushy feeling in the pit of your stomach. But what happens when that emotion leaves you? And, trust me, it probably will after a while.

Sometimes love is harder than we think.

Love can make you smile and feel like you could float on air. Yet love can break your heart and cause your tears to fall. Love can be a struggle in your heart that leaves you exhausted.

But love can also change the world.

When I felt God lead me to include a chapter on love in this book, I felt inadequate to write it. To be honest, I didn't *want* to write it. I am in no way perfect in the area of showing unconditional love to others, and I can really struggle with this at times. I don't think that any of us will ever be *perfect* in this area, but I do think that the more we extend unconditional love to others, the easier it will become.

I have always been one to love deeply and when someone would betray or hurt me, I hurt deeply.

For almost fourteen years of my life, my mother raised my twin sister and I on her own. She worked hard to provide for us as a single parent and to teach us about God. I would not be writing this right now—I would not be who I am today—if it weren't for my mom.

When I was thirteen, my mom married my wonderful step-dad. He was the father I prayed for every night and so much more.

But for years in my life there was bitterness deep in my heart for my biological father who left my mom when she was pregnant. I was angry with him for the things he did not only to me, but to my mom and sister. I tried to forget about what happened and I tried to forgive him, but I was hurting so much that I just couldn't seem to let it go.

Of course I knew all the right things to do. I knew what I needed to say. I knew what the Bible said.

*"But I say to you who hear: Love your enemies, do good to those who hate you, bless those who curse you, and pray for those who spitefully use you."*

*~Luke 6:27-28*

*"Beloved, let us love one another, for love is of God; and everyone who loves is born of God and knows God. He who does not love does not know God, for God is love. In this the love of God was manifested toward us, that God has sent His only begotten Son into the world, that we might live through Him. In this is love, not that we loved God, but that He loved us and sent His Son to be the propitiation for our sins. Beloved, if God so loved us, we also ought to love one another."*

*~1 John 4:7-11*

*"A new commandment I give to you, that you love one another; as I have loved you, that you also love one another. By this all will know that you are My disciples, if you have love for one another."*

*~John 13:34-35*

Yet somehow these verses seemed so much harder to follow in the moments when hurtful memories from the past continued to remain at the front of my mind.

*I don't want to do it,* I argued to God. *I can't do it.*

Isn't that how it usually goes though?

We act so strong when things are going great. "Yeah, I can do that. I can forgive those who hurt me and show them unconditional love. I can do that, no problem."

And then a friend's betrayal cuts our heart a little too deeply. A parent's absence wounds a little too much. A teacher's words belittle you too often.

On and on the list goes.

I think that at some point in time in their life, everyone who ever lived on this earth suffered hurt from someone else. They suffered pain from loving someone who didn't show them love back. Even Jesus suffered the betrayal of a friend who had followed Him for years.

And that is when we begin to wonder if showing unconditional love to others really is possible or even worth it.

After all, the more we love the more we're going to get hurt, right? I mean, that's what our world today tells us. Only love someone if you can get something out of it and make sure *you* hurt *them* before *they* hurt *you*.

This may be what the world tells us, but it's not what God tells us to do.

Look again at the verses mentioned above.

Love—unconditional love—is what sets us as Christians apart from the world. We are to love our enemies. Do good to those who hate us, those who hurt us over and over. Bless those who curse us, those who mock us and make fun of us day after day. Pray for those who spitefully use us, those who pretend to love us only to get what they want and then they hurt us.

No exceptions.

As world-changers and difference-makers, God is calling us to be different from the world. God is calling us to do something so radically different from what the world teaches that people will have no choice but to take notice.

No, it's not easy. I mean, how can it be easy to love someone who hurts you? How can it be easy to forgive someone who hurts those you love? How can it be easy to show love unconditionally, no matter the cost?

But just because it isn't easy, doesn't mean that you can't do it.

With God all things are possible (Matthew 19:26). We can do all things through Christ who strengthens us (Philippians 4:13).

As I struggled with my feelings of bitterness and even hatred for my biological father, I began to feel God leading me to forgive him and show him love, even if nothing in me wanted to do it. And there wasn't *anything* in me that wanted to do what God was asking of me.

Yet during that time not too long ago, I began to read over a fiction novel that I had written a couple years earlier. The story is about teen missionaries in Uganda (*of course* that's where they had to go!), and throughout the book they learn what it means to show unconditional love to others.

I was only skimming through the pages, but towards the end my eyes were drawn to words that were spoken by one of my main characters, Faith.

*"All it takes is love. A love that only God can give to us. A love that can change the world."*

*A love that can change the world.*

I stared at those words for a long time and I felt led by God to share them with you on these pages right now.

The whole purpose of this book is to encourage you to use your life for God's glory and to make a difference in your world. All of that is great.

But if you truly want to change your world, you need to start by unconditionally loving other people.

As I was contemplating this, a hard question kept coming back to my mind. *Do I love Jesus more than I hate what my biological father did to me?*

And that's the point.

We need to love and forgive others, not just because it will bring us freedom, but because we love Jesus more.

Jesus is our perfect example of what beautiful, unconditional love looks like.

I mean, after all, He died for us! He died for us when we were still sinning (Romans 5:8). He died for us even as we turned our backs on Him and went on living our own way. He loves us so much that nothing we have done or will do can change that amazing love. Reflect on that for a moment.

I honestly believe that if we do not know Christ and His love for us, we cannot give to others that unconditional love, because as I said before: it is a love that only God can give to us to give away to others.

The reason that the world out there is telling you that you need to only love those who love you back, is because without God's love in your life, you would have no reason to love others.

But when we know God's love and we let it fill our hearts, we realize that we can't keep it to ourselves. It was meant to give away to others. It was meant to give away just as unconditionally as it was given to us.

If you do not know God's love for you, please read the gospel story in the Bible that tells about Christ's death on the cross for *us*, because He loved *us*. He loved *you*.

Once you accept God's love, learn to love Him back. When you love Him with all of your heart, it will be easier to show love to others.

Will the love that you extend to others hurt sometimes? Yes, I'm sure it will. Will you sometimes want to give up? Yes, I'm sure of it.

But you must *never give up*.

That day when I read the words I had written, "A love that can change the world," God asked me whether or not I was going to give His love away to others who hurt me, or whether I was going to pass up the opportunity to change my world. Even though it hurt and I didn't *feel* like I could do it, I begged God to place a love and forgiveness in my heart that could only come from Him. With the help of God I am continuing to choose that love, but it is a choice I have to make every day.

Before I go any further however, I want to make one thing very clear.

If you are in a physically or emotionally abusive relationship, you do not have to stay in that relationship. You can show love and forgiveness from afar. If you are in such a situation I encourage you to seek help from a trusted adult.

Although I forgave my biological father, I have chosen not to see him so that I do not put myself in a situation that could be emotionally damaging to me in the future.

Sometimes it is necessary to walk away from a relationship that is not physically, emotionally, or spiritually helpful to you. If a friend continually puts you down and hurts you, maybe it's time to say that you love her/him, but you can't hang out anymore. If a parent abuses you, it's time to get help for them and yourself, showing them love and forgiveness from a distance. If a boyfriend or girlfriend asks you to go against your beliefs, it's time to walk away from the relationship.

Not all relationships are good to be in, and hopefully your Bible and a trusted adult can help you distinguish which situations you need to continue to show love in, and which ones you need to walk away from lovingly.

Another area that is important if you want to change your world is learning to forgive *yourself*. Just as you have to learn to forgive others who have wronged you, you also must be able to forgive yourself. If you hold your past mistakes and failures close, you will only hinder further progress in making a difference.

I remember when God called me to fight human trafficking, I was so angry with myself for the areas where I felt I had failed to do something and I would not forgive myself for those times. What I realized was that those feelings of bitterness towards myself were only causing me to stay stuck where I was. They were not allowing me to be able to move forward with my vision and my passion.

Learn to let things go. Some people say, "Forgive and forget." But I don't think that you will ever truly be able to *forget* things that happened in the past. You just need to learn how to not allow the past to control your present and future. Do not dwell on things that happened in the past, but instead choose to learn from your mistakes and the mistakes of others.

Changing the world through unconditional love is something God invented a *long* time ago. Since the creation of the world, His plan was to change our lives, one by one, through the power of the unconditional love of Jesus Christ.

I believe that God wants us to be a part of His plan to use unconditional love to change the world. I believe that His plan all along was to change us through His beautiful love, and then have us go out into our homes, communities, and world, changing the lives of others through that love. Sometimes we are the only image of Christ's love that non-believers see. I think that they are watching us, wondering if we truly believe that God's love can change the world. And if we do believe that, then we know that we can give that love away to others, no matter how much it hurts sometimes.

What do you need to start doing today to show unconditional love to someone?

Maybe you need to forgive a parent who left a long time ago. Maybe you need to show kindness to those friends who hurt you, or reach out to those outcasts in your school and church who need a friend. Maybe you need to stop judging others just because they look differently or dress differently than you do. Maybe you need to grow closer to God so that you can be filled with His unconditional love.

Whatever it is that you need to do to change your world through love, *I dare you* to go out and do it. You never know what that one, simple act of love can do to change someone's life.

And before I close this chapter, I want to share with you a story I wrote about choosing to love others...no matter what the cost.


## *The Cost of Love*

*A Story...*

*The day that dawned* upon a busy city in California was nothing short of breathtakingly beautiful.

The brilliantly blue sky was dotted occasionally with white, puffy clouds that floated past the shining sun. The breeze was cool, a welcome relief from the heat of the sun's rays.

The birds chirped a harmonious melody as the dragonflies buzzed past. Butterflies drifted on the breeze happily. The sweet aroma of the flowers, that provided a splash of color amongst the green grass, wafted through the air.

In a small neighborhood, children played and giggled while fathers mowed the lawn or stopped to greet one another after picking up the mail.

At the end of a winding driveway sat a two-story brick home. The white porch wrapped around the house, while pink and blue pansies in wooden baskets hung from the tall pillars.

The windows of the house were thrown open wide to let in the cool breeze, and the smell of freshly cut grass drifted inside.

In a bedroom on the second floor a young girl sat cross-legged on her bed. The walls were painted pink, purple, and blue, and the light radiating from the sun created a bright atmosphere.

Sixteen-year-old Jenna Reyes stared out the window that was accented by white, frilly curtains. A soft smile played on her ruby lips as she brushed a strand of her auburn curls from her emerald eyes.

*I love summer!* She sighed to herself. She slowly sat up and climbed off her bed. Picking up her Bible she gently placed it on her desk, leaving it open to 1 John where she had been studying.

She skipped happily to the hallway and down the maple staircase. Once in the kitchen she picked up the telephone and dialed a number quickly.

*"Hello, this is Olivia Mitchell! I'm sorry I can't pick up my phone right now, but leave a message and I'll call you back. God bless!"*

Jenna sighed. "Hi, Sis, it's Jen. Call me back when you get the chance. Mom went to the grocery store, Dad's at work, and I'm at home. Talk to you later. Love you."

She silently hung up the phone, sad that her adored older sister had not answered.

Olivia was four years older than Jenna, and growing up Jen had loved having an older sister. It had been bittersweet for her when Olivia got married two years earlier. She hardly ever saw her sister anymore, especially now that Olivia and her husband, Luke, had their first child.

Jenna pushed aside her sadness and skipped outside. Her mood was bright as she walked down the driveway towards the mailbox. She reached in and pulled the mail out, briefly skimming through it. Disappointed that she didn't have a pen pal letter, she began to head back towards the house.

Suddenly a silver van swerved up against the sidewalk, barely missing the curb.

Jenna jumped back quickly and gasped. It took her a moment to realize that it was her mom's van. She ran to the open window of the van and looked inside.

Fear seized her heart at the sight of her mother's wide eyes and pale face.

"What's wrong?" she asked, panic washing over her body and her knees feeling weak.

"It's your sister," her mother gasped out, tears beginning to stream down her face.

Jenna felt her heart skip a beat and everything seemed to happen in slow motion. She gasped for breath. "What happened to her?" she demanded, flinging open the van door and sliding in.

The instant the door closed, Mrs. Reyes pulled the vehicle away from the sidewalk and sped off down the road.

"Mom, please tell me what happened!" Jenna begged her mother. Her knuckles were white as she clutched the dashboard in front of her.

Mrs. Reye's eyes flooded with tears again. "Olivia was driving home and a truck hit her head-on. The driver of the truck was on his phone. Your father called me because the police called him at work. They said it doesn't look good."

Jenna felt her blood run cold as sobs threatened to spill out of her. Her sister was in a car accident? It didn't look good? *Oh, Lord Jesus, please don't take my sister. Please, save her!*

She whipped her head around to stare at her mother. "She didn't have the baby with her, did she? Please tell me Faith wasn't with her!"

Mrs. Reyes patted her daughter's hand gently. "No, Faith was at home with Luke." Her jaw clenched as she turned onto the main road.

The rest of the trip to the hospital was in silence as Jenna and her mother fought back tears. With every beat of her heart she begged God to save her sister's life.

Everything went past in a blur for Jenna as she followed her mother into the hospital lobby and up to the second floor.

Coming out of the elevator, her eyes instantly glanced around. Panic overwhelmed her when she caught sight of Luke leaning against the wall, holding Faith and weeping bitterly.

Mr. Reyes looked up and was at his wife's side in an instant. He wrapped his arms around her as she sobbed and her knees gave way underneath her.

"What happened?" Jenna demanded her arms outstretched. A feeling of dread entered the pit of her stomach.

Her father glanced at her, his eyes glassy from tears. "We lost her." A fresh burst of sobs from her mother interrupted him.

Jenna felt dizzy as her head began to spin. She leaned against the wall and slid to her knees. She was too stunned to cry. None of her father's words seemed real.

"I didn't get to say goodbye," she whispered. "I didn't get to tell her how much I love her."

She looked up quickly when her brother-in-law placed a hand on her shoulder. "She knew how much you loved her," he whispered. "She loved you just as much."

Jenna felt hot tears stinging her eyes as she stood up and stroked Faith's soft, chubby cheek. "It wasn't even her fault. Why'd she have to die?" she sobbed out loud.

"We lost the baby too."

Jenna jerked her head up and stared at her father as if he had grown two heads. "What baby?" she asked in a high-pitched voice, another wave of panic washing over her.

"We were going to tell you tonight when we came over to your house for dinner," Luke whispered as he rocked his baby daughter back and forth, a look of sheer pain on his face.

"Olivia was pregnant."

~~~~~~

*Five weeks later...*

Jenna sighed as she leaned back against the numerous pillows on her bed. A hot tear slowly slipped from the corner of her eye. She sniffed and rolled onto her side. Faith lay beside her, sleeping soundly.

She gave a half-smile as she leaned over to kiss the seven-month-old's check. She loved being an aunt. A sharp pain pierced her heart at the thought. Her next little niece or nephew was gone and so was her older sister. She had never felt so much grief in her heart before.

"Jen," a gentle voice whispered.

Jenna rolled over to see her mother standing in her bedroom doorway. She forced a smile. "Hi, Mom," she whispered back.

Mrs. Reyes smiled as she came over to wipe the stray curls from her daughter's forehead.

"Luke is here," she explained. "Your father and I are heading out to the Tyler's home. Luke said he can watch Faith if you would like to come with us."

Jenna got a confused look on her face. "Who are the Tyler's?" She recognized the name, but her memory was so foggy from the grief that she couldn't remember how she knew them.

Mrs. Reyes took a deep breath. "You remember, don't you? Mr. Tyler was killed in the same accident your sister was."

Jenna's pulse quickened and hatred washed over her. She sat up so quickly her head began to spin.

"You mean the Mr. Tyler that *killed my sister*?" she asked, trying to keep her voice calm.

Mrs. Reyes nodded slowly. "Jen, the Tyler's are hurting right now too. Mrs. Tyler's husband was killed and her children's father. I know what you must be feeling though, honey."

"Mom!" Jenna interjected. "It wasn't like it was an accident, an innocent mistake. He was texting! He killed

Livy and her baby!" Sobs threatened to overtake her as her shoulders began to shake.

Mrs. Reyes placed both hands on her daughter's shoulders. "Jenna, honey, Livy was my daughter. I was heartbroken when I found out that her and the baby…" her voice trailed off. She closed her eyes and mouthed a silent prayer. Her eyes slowly opened again and stared deeply into her youngest daughter's. "I was so angry at first and I hated Mr. Tyler for what he did. But, despite the fact that my pain is still very deep, I know that I cannot keep that hatred and anger inside of me. Yes, Mr. Tyler was wrong. But the people who killed Jesus were wrong too! And, sweetie, He forgave them. How can we do any less?"

Jenna looked away, shaking her head. "I'm not going with you," she whispered softly, pain and anger piercing her heart.

Mrs. Reyes sighed. "Fine. I'll call you when we are on our way back, okay?"

Jenna nodded as she wrapped her arms around herself. "Love you, Mom."

Mrs. Reyes kissed her daughter's forehead. "I love you, Jenna."

Jenna watched in silence as her mother picked up Faith and left the room quietly.

All alone, the room held an eerie silence. Her heart was beating so loudly that it echoed in her ears.

Finally she let the sobs pour out. She rocked back and forth as she sobbed and gasped for air.

"God, why'd You take her?" she cried out, her heart breaking. "I'm hurting so badly right now. Please, help me!"

**"I love you, Jen."**

Jenna began to cry harder as she realized how much God *did* love her. Her pain eased slightly as she slid to her knees.

**"I love the Tyler's too."**

Jenna felt her heart skip a beat as her head jerked up. "But, God, he killed Livy and the baby! He killed my sweet, innocent sister!"

**"I know it hurts. But I love them, and I want you to love them too."**

Jenna shook her head vigorously as she jumped up and began to pace the room, her feet feeling heavy, like a piece of metal was strapped to them.

The day outside was bright and cheery, just as it had been the day her world changed.

But this time nothing in her felt cheery or happy.

The bright sun and the cheerful laughter of neighbor children playing seemed out of place in her world that was still dark with grief and pain.

Looking over to her desk briefly, she noticed her Bible lying open, the same place she had left it five weeks earlier.

Slowly, she ran her fingers across the words of 1 John.

Next to her Bible lay another Bible, the beautiful name of Olivia Jane Reyes inscribed on the front.

She smiled at the memory of her beloved sister. She slowly opened the worn pages of Olivia's Bible. The pages slid open to a chapter in Matthew. Tucked in between the pages was a small letter on pink paper that was decorated with colorful flowers.

Her heart pounding, she picked up the letter and opened it. Tears flooded her eyes at her sister's familiar handwriting. The note was dated two days before the accident that took her life.

*Dear Jen,*

*It's me, your big sister. ☺ I wanted to write you a quick note today to let you know some things the Lord has been teaching me in my Bible study. In Matthew 5:44 we are told; "But I say to you, love your enemies, bless those who curse you, do good to those who hate you, and pray for those who spitefully use you and persecute you."*

*The Lord has been teaching me about this a lot. When people hurt us or others we love it is very difficult to love them. But Jesus tells us to! Loving our enemies or those who have wronged us is hard but God is our strength, my dear sister! We also must forgive those who have wronged us. Luke 23:34 says—"Then Jesus said, 'Father, forgive them, for they do not know what they do.' And they divided His garments and cast lots."*

*These verses mean a lot to me because it shows how much Jesus loves us. He not only forgave us, but He prayed for His Father to forgive us too. If He can forgive and love me, how can I do any less?*

*Well, I must go for now, but keep these verses close to your heart, Jenna. He will guide you!*

*All my love always,*
*Olivia*

Through blurry vision, Jenna looked up from the beautiful letter, clutching it closely to her heart. Instantly, her eyes landed on the words of 1 John, in chapter four.

*"In this is love, not that we loved God, but that He loved us and sent His Son to be the propitiation for our sins. Beloved, if God so loved us, we also ought to love one another."*

Sobs began to shake Jenna's body as the words sunk in. She crumbled to her knees, clutching the precious letter from her sister close to her heart.

"Thank You, Jesus," she prayed aloud. "Thank You so much. I've been so wrong. Help me to love like You love me. Please, Jesus, be my strength. Help me do what I know I need to do."

~~~~~~~

"Are you sure you're ready to do this?" Mrs. Reyes asked her daughter gently the following morning.

Jenna smiled as she opened the van door. "God will give me strength. Thanks for driving me, Mom."

"I'll be back in an hour, okay?" her mother promised.

Jenna waved as she watched the van drive out of her sight. She took a deep breath and tucked her hand into her skirt pocket, clutching the note her sister had given her and the verses from 1 John.

She stared at the unfamiliar house in front of her, her heart pounding. *Lord Jesus, help me...*

With shaking hands she knocked on the front door. Within seconds a middle-aged women answered the door.

"Hello," she asked, her eyes looking tired. "Can I help you?"

Jenna swallowed hard and smiled. "My name is Jenna Reyes," she began.

The women's eyes grew wide and her fingers clutched the doorknob tighter. "Jenna!" she gasped.

Jenna nodded. "You must be Mrs. Tyler, right?"

The women nodded. "Yes," she answered, tears filling her eyes. "Honey, I'm so sorry for what happened. My husband wasn't a bad man; he just did something wrong. I'm so sorry." Silent sobs began to shake her shoulders.

Jenna stood there, unsure of what to do. Slowly, she reached her arms out to hug Mrs. Tyler. Tears filled her own eyes as she prayed silently. Love flooded over her heart and she no longer felt dragged down by the feelings of hatred she had been carrying for so long.

Mrs. Tyler pulled away gently and smiled. "Thank you, thank you so much, Jenna. Is there a reason you came here today?"

Jenna smiled back. "Actually, yes there is. I noticed that your lawn needs mowed. Would you mind if I did it for you? And I also brought some games to play with your children later."

Mrs. Tyler gasped. "Why are doing this? Why do you forgive us?" Tears trembled on her eyelashes.

"Because Someone very wonderful forgave and loved me first. Why don't I tell you about Him while I get the lawn mower ready?" she suggested, beginning to relax.

Mrs. Tyler nodded as she opened the door for Jenna to step in.

Jenna walked in, her step feeling lighter. *Thank You, Jesus for forgiving me and loving me. Thank You for giving me the strength to give that love to the Tyler's. You truly are an awesome God!*

With a smile on her lips she began to tell Mrs. Tyler about the unconditional love that God gave to her so many years ago and how it changed her life.

~~~~~~~

*"For God so loved the world that He gave His only begotten Son, that whoever believes in Him should not perish but have everlasting life."*

*~John 3:16~*

# Chapter Eight

*I Dare You to Believe the Impossible...*

# Chapter 8:
## I Dare You to Believe the Impossible

*My God is a miracle-working God.*

I don't care how many times someone tells me that something is impossible. I don't care how many times it is said that something can't be done. Every time, I will stand up tall and say five simple words:

*My God still works miracles.*

When we are young we believe that we can do anything. If you don't believe me, think back to when you were seven years old. If at that age the thought ever crossed your mind that one day you were going to fly to the moon, then at that time you *did* believe in the impossible. I mean, one day you could actually fly to the moon, but I can guarantee you that it won't be as easy as you thought it would be when you were seven.

One of the special things about youth is the innocence that goes with it. The innocence that doesn't realize that there are things that maybe we can't accomplish. The innocence that believes what God tells us to do, no matter how difficult the circumstance may be.

Kids used to have this faith even through their teenage years until they became an adult. But sadly I have noticed that, as time goes on, we have begun to lose our simple, gonna-fly-to-the-moon faith as soon as we begin to grow up.

Sooner and sooner we begin to listen to what the world tells us.

*That's impossible. You're too young to do something like that. That can't be done. Be realistic.*

I don't know about you, but I'm tired of listening to those lies.

As you know, I was almost eleven when God called me to go to Uganda. I was young at the time, and in my heart I knew that my calling was to go to Africa.

At the time, the only things I knew for certain were that I was not going to be able to go until I was older, but that I *was* going to go.

I had no idea how I was going to get there. I had no idea what I was going to do when I got there. And I had no idea how I was going to make a difference in a country so beautiful, but in so much need.

I just knew that God wanted me to go and I truly believed that if He called me there, He was going to make a way.

As I grew up, God made some things clearer for me. He gave me a clearer vision of what I wanted to do in Uganda and how I was going to get there.

No, I still don't have it all figured out and I'm pretty sure that I won't know the whole plan until I actually get there. But I was always okay with that because I believed that God works miracles and He could use me however He wanted to.

Yet, sometime along the way I began to lose the innocent faith I had when I was eleven.

Well-meaning adults began to tell me that I needed to have a plan, I needed to be realistic. In my heart I began to doubt things God had told me.

*What if I wasn't being realistic? What if I had believed in something that was impossible? What if I wasn't meant to go to Uganda after all? What if some things just couldn't be done?*

And then I realized something.

Throughout the Bible you read of the miracles God performed. From the Old Testament to the New Testament, God looks out for the needs of His people and when things seem impossible, He always makes a way.

He parted the sea. He let manna rain down from heaven. He destroyed a city with a simple shout.

And on and on the examples go.

It was then that I began to wonder.

Why do we live our lives as if God can no longer perform crazy, unbelievable miracles? Why do we brush certain things off as impossible? Do we not believe that our God is still a miracle-working God?

I think it's time that this generation wakes up. God is still God! He is the same yesterday, today, and *forever!* He never changes! He can do whatever He wants to do. If He wants to tell me to go to Uganda and just trust Him for some of the details, then I can fully believe that He will provide, even if it's in miraculous ways.

If He tells you to do something impossible for His glory, then you go out and do it, trusting Him for the results.

And if anyone tells you that you're not being realistic, tell them that God doesn't always use realistic.

I'm pretty sure that Moses didn't think it realistic to stretch out his hand across the Red Sea and separate the waters so that they could all walk through on dry ground.

I'm pretty sure that David didn't think it realistic to kill a giant with a slingshot and small stone. If that were

141

me, I would have been begging God to give me a shield at least.

I'm pretty sure Gideon didn't think it realistic when God told him to defeat the Midianites with three hundred men and a couple trumpets.

I'm pretty sure that Mary didn't think it realistic when an angel told her that she was going to have a baby—*the Son of God*—when she was a virgin.

I'm pretty sure that the disciples didn't think it realistic that Jesus was going to be their Savior and King when He died on the cross and was placed in a tomb.

But in every single one of these stories, God performs a miracle.

He uses the weaknesses, the insufficiencies of others, the unlikely choices to change the course of history and make His power and glory known to a lost world.

It is true that in today's world you don't hear very many stories of people walking through the sea on dry ground, but I believe that is partly our fault.

It seems as if the generations today have no faith in the impossible at all. If something seems a little scary, outside our comfort zone, or unrealistic, we better not even attempt it because if we fail we will surely be looked upon in the wrong way.

And I believe that this is the reason that we do not see as many miracles in our world today as we could. Yes, there are miracle stories out there and I believe that those things happen to those who have a faith that is not limited.

*"And Jesus rebuked the demon, and it came out of him; and the child was cured from that very hour. Then the disciples came to Jesus privately and said, 'Why could we not cast it*

*out?' So Jesus said to them, 'Because of your unbelief; for assuredly, I say to you, if you have faith as a mustard seed, you will say to this mountain, 'Move from here to there,' and it will move; and nothing will be impossible for you.'"*

~Matthew 17:18-20

Faith as small as a mustard seed.

Have any of you ever seen a mustard seed?

Well, they're small. Like *really* small.

Is it possible that our faith has become so limited that we don't even have enough to reach the size of a mustard seed? We're completely fine with things that we can see or that we can control on our own. If something seems a little challenging, but we can handle it in our own strength, then we are okay to attempt it.

But when it comes to trusting God to do the impossible, things are a little bit different.

And is it even more possible that we are looking over the miracles God gives us every day because maybe they aren't bread raining down from heaven?

I truly believe that in order to make a difference in the world, we have to get back to the limitless faith we had when we were seven.

I know that God can still perform miracles and, in fact, I think that He is just waiting for someone to trust Him enough to perform them.

I have seen God give my family miracles or make a way in an impossible circumstance. I have seen Him come through for me when I had the faith to pray and trust Him.

I was always afraid that if I attempted to do something that was impossible, I would look like a fool if

I failed and people would laugh at me or make fun of me.

If you remember in chapter two, I shared with you my idea of having a benefit concert to raise money to end slavery. Music has always been one of my favorite things in the world, so this seemed like a great idea to me.

Yes, perhaps I was slightly ambitious because I tried to ask a very popular singer to do the concert, but I honestly believed that God could make it happen. Despite the advice I was given that maybe I should start out smaller, I decided to shoot for the stars. I was slightly nervous that the plans would fail and people would laugh, but I realized something.

We are not the ones performing the miracle.

We are not the ones doing the impossible.

We have the faith and God does the rest. Yes, He uses us, but it's not really us who are performing miracles. Moses was used to stretch out his hand across the Red Sea, but he's not the one who parted the waters.

Since I wasn't the one going to actually do the impossible, I knew that it was okay if it didn't work out. Yes, I would be a part of it, but it would not have been entirely in my strength.

If the concert happened, it would be God that people would look to and realize that He was the One to get the glory. He could handle the situation, and if He wanted to let the concert happen, He could've made a way. If He didn't let it happen, He could handle that situation too.

Just because He chose not to let it happen, doesn't mean that I didn't have enough faith. Trust me; if you saw me before my mom made the call to the singer's booking agent, you would've known that I had a *lot* of faith. What it meant was that He had other ideas in mind.

He wanted me to make a difference some other way. He wanted me to believe that He is still a miracle-working God even when things didn't go my way and I didn't get the miracle I wanted.

I also realized that maybe God wanted me to go to local bands that He could use to make a difference. And you never know, I can be very persistent, so maybe He'll decide to let me get a major band come one of these days.

Either way, I still believe that He can work miracles.

And He can do it for you too.

What is it that you want to accomplish for Him? Does it seem impossible? Are people telling you that it isn't realistic?

If so, maybe it's time to go to God. Ask Him to make a way where there may seem to be no way. Turn it over to Him and stop trying to do it all in your own strength.

In Numbers 20, we see the story of how Moses was told by God to speak to a rock and water would pour out of it for the people of Israel to drink. Moses, however, didn't have enough faith, so instead he hit the rock twice. God still performed the miracle and let water come out, but Moses was then not allowed to go into the Promised Land with the rest of Israel.

We can't do the impossible on our own. And we can't do it our own way.

Why? Because changing the world and watching God do the impossible is never about *us*. It is *always* about Him and His power and glory. It's about what He chooses to do with those who are committed to having faith in Him no matter what.

Do what God asks of you and when the miracle happens, give Him all the glory. Maybe Moses did what he did because he wanted the glory for the miracle.

Maybe he did it because he didn't believe that God could do it. I don't know, but what I do know is that we need to believe in the God of the impossible and how He wants to change the world.

When you begin to pursue the dreams that God has placed on your heart, you will come across situations that are impossible. At those times, pray and ask God for a way to make it happen. If He gives it to you, that's great. If not, that's okay too, because I know that He will show up in some other way that is even greater than you ever imagined.

I wanted to share with you one more Scripture passage that speaks about what God can do with those who believe in Him:

*"Most assuredly, I say to you, he who believes in Me, the works that I do he will do also; and greater works than these he will do, because I go to My Father. And whatever you ask in My name, that I will do, that the Father may be glorified in the Son. If you ask anything in My name, I will do it."*

*~John 14:12-14*

Jesus promises to do the impossible in our lives for the glory of God our Father. When we pray according to *His will*, in His name, He will always come through in mighty, powerful ways, even if it isn't how we wanted.

You might not always see it instantly, but I believe that you will see a miracle. I dare you to believe it to.

I dare you to, no matter what happens, always believe in the impossible and the God who makes miracles happen.

Before I close this chapter, I want to share with you my story of when I competed at the 2013 National Bible

Bee. To me, some of the ways that God answered my prayers were miracles. Now these circumstances weren't *impossible*, but I know that it was something that I could have *never* done on my own strength. I hope that this story of how God answered my prayers in unbelievable ways for me will encourage you to trust Him with *your* prayers. I hope it will encourage you to believe in the power of prayer.

## *My 2013 National Bible Bee Testimony*

I stared at the locked computer screen, my heart pounding in my ears.

It was August 28th, 2013 at 8:16pm and I was sitting in my youth pastor's office at my church. I was certain that I would remain calm at this moment, but so far my nerves got the better of me.

"I think you made it!" my friend eagerly informed me.

I couldn't help but smile. "I didn't do the Bible Bee to make Nationals, so whatever my score is, I will praise God." Closing my eyes, I added, *Thank You, Jesus. Thank You for all You've already done for me. I'm so grateful. To You be the glory forever and ever!*

It hadn't been long since I had competed at my local Bible Bee where I placed 2nd in the senior division by the grace of God. However, to advance to the national competition that November, my oral and written scores from the local contest would have to place me in the top 120 from the nation.

I was nervous to say the least, but a strange peace filled my heart at the same time. The previous months of study for the local competition were memories that filled my thoughts that night. Even if I didn't make Nationals, I knew that I would never trade those hours that I spent immersed in God's Word. It had been such a special summer for me and I did the Bible Bee completely for the glory of God and to know Him better.

At that moment, my youth pastor entered the room. With a smile, he unlocked the computer and I quickly began to type the Bible Bee website into the Internet browser.

It didn't take long before I brought up the website and found where the local scores had been posted. I tried to calm my breathing as I typed in my contestant I.D. and age division.

When my scores came up, the whole room erupted in everyone screaming and talking at once. I probably screamed the loudest as grateful tears filled my eyes.

I had placed 85th in the nation, qualifying me for Nationals.

I was beyond grateful and I could only continue to give God all the glory and praise for it. I had not done it in my own strength and I knew that it was only because of Him that I had made it this far.

I had no idea, however, just how many more surprises God had in store for me in the coming months.

As I studied for Nationals, there were days when I grew weary and tired. Yet it was as if God was eager to give me His strength to keep going.

When I made it to Nationals on November 20, 2013 in Tennessee, I felt as if it were a miracle that God had chosen to give me. And I couldn't have been more excited to see what He had in store.

The fellowship of Nationals with so many other amazing friends and fellow contestants was beyond encouraging for me. On November 21st, I would again take an oral and written test.

That morning I was awake before the sun came up, praying for two hours as I asked God to give me His peace for the coming day. I prayed for three specific things that morning before heading down to the convention center for my written test.

First, I asked Him to help me to know at least most of the written test questions. The local written test had been very difficult and I was hoping that I had studied enough to make this test a bit easier.

Next, I prayed that I would not be afraid *at all* during my oral test. I knew this would be the most difficult for me, but I didn't want to be nervous at all. I didn't care whether or not I made mistakes. I told God that I would be okay with it if I messed up every single verse. I just didn't want to be nervous.

Finally, I asked my Jesus to please let my favorite verse, Philippians 3:8-11, to be the first verse I quoted in my oral test. I had my doubts however that this would be the first verse, let alone be asked at all during the test.

Throughout the day, God showed up in ways that, to me, were a miracle.

Things that I seriously didn't think would happen, God came through and let them happen.

My written test was first and my heart rate was only increased slightly as that hour began. I finished early, surprised by how easy the test seemed. Out of the 200 questions, there were only about 45 questions that I was completely unsure of. This was a big difference from the local test and, to be honest, I was so surprised by how easy it seemed that I almost cried! I could've jumped with excitement.

Going into my oral test, however, my excitement level began to decrease. My hands were trembling and I could hardly speak without my voice shaking. I was incredibly disappointed that I was nervous and I asked God why I had to be afraid. The nerves only escalated when I stood in front of my two judges.

"We want to get a feel for how loudly you quote before the test begins, so would you please quote for us your favorite verse?" one of my judges asked with a smile before my actual oral test began.

I was so stunned that I just stared at her for a minute. In the three years that I had done Bible Bee, they had never asked me to do this before the oral test.

"Like *any* verse?" I asked, trying to hide my shock.

Tears shone in my eyes as I began to quote Philippians 3:8-11. I looked up to heaven as I spoke the familiar words and instantly my nerves left. I did not feel afraid or nervous at all. To me, this was a miracle that God gave me to show me how much He loves me and it still brings me to tears as I write these words. I didn't think this prayer would be answered, and I truly regretted my unbelief.

My oral test began and I stumbled on my first verse. I left several words out and continued to ask for prompts during the next few passages. Despite the fact that I wasn't really doing that well, I couldn't stop smiling. I wasn't nervous and I was actually having so much fun! I was even kind of sad when the test ended.

That day was truly one that I will never forget for the rest of my life. That night at the Opening Ceremony, I found out that I was not in the top 15, so I wasn't a semi-finalist.

I knew many of the finalists however and I couldn't have been more happy for them or proud. I stood up and smiled. Closing my eyes, I knew in my heart that the over 850 hours that I had spent since June in my Bible Bee study were not in vain. They were all worth it to know Jesus more deeply and He was my reward.

That December I found out that my oral and written scores had placed me 55th amongst the National qualifiers. This was a complete shock to me and something that I thought couldn't happen. I didn't believe that I could place that well, especially after how awful my oral test was. It was yet again another sweet surprise that God gave me.

I couldn't help but smile and close my eyes again, thinking back over the wonderful time I had during the Bible Bee and my intense study.

With tears streaming down my cheeks, I whispered to Jesus the words that had become the anthem of my life: "I count it all as loss compared to knowing You, Father. You are *worth it all.*"

*Soli Deo Gloria—To God alone be the glory always!*

*"But Jesus looked at them and said, 'With men it is impossible, but not with God; for with God all things are possible.'"*

*~Mark 10:27~*

# Chapter Nine

*I Dare You to Never Back Down...*

# Chapter 9:
## I Dare You to Never Back Down

*"Why don't you eat chocolate?"*

The question came at me and I couldn't help but smile. I still love answering this question when people ask because it gives me the opportunity to share with others a passion that is very close to my heart.

As I write these words, it has been about three and a half years since I first found out about slavery and human trafficking in our world. I first read about slavery that taints the chocolate that most of us consume. (For more information on this, read chapter ten.)

When I found out about this for the first time, my heart was utterly broken. I wanted to do something and so I did the only thing I knew to do.

I gave up eating chocolate unless I knew that it was 100% fairly traded.

This wasn't exactly easy for me at the time because I *loved* chocolate, especially chocolate ice cream. And seriously, who doesn't like chocolate peanut butter cups?

But I knew in my heart that giving it up was the right thing to do. It was a year before I got my first fair trade chocolate bar and I just recently got to try fair trade chocolate ice cream (I was so excited that the people in the food store probably thought I was crazy).

But there were a lot of times throughout the past few years when I would choose to not eat chocolate because it wasn't fair trade. I was questioned about this a lot and most people usually smiled, but weren't that interested.

It was about a year after I gave up chocolate that someone I knew asked me, "Why don't you eat chocolate?"

"I only eat fairly traded cocoa because I believe that we can do something to end slavery, even if it's a really small thing to do," was my fast, rehearsed response.

This person didn't believe that slavery existed in most of the chocolate that we consume.

"Even if it did, what possible difference do you think *you're* making by giving it up? Someone else will just eat it and you won't be making a difference at all."

I was unsure of how to respond to that comment and so I politely walked away.

But that day I began to wonder what possible difference I *was* making.

I mean, most people in the world eat chocolate. Even if I gave it up there was no way that I could be helping this problem, right?

And then I came across the story in the Bible of how Jesus fed over 5,000 people. This story became special to me, so I'd like to share it with you.

*"Then Jesus lifted up His eyes, and seeing a great multitude coming toward Him, He said to Philip, 'Where shall we buy bread, that these may eat?'*

*But this He said to test him, for He Himself knew what He would do.*

*Philip answered Him, 'Two hundred denarii worth of bread is not sufficient for them, that every one of them may have a little.'*

One of His disciples, Andrew, Simon Peter's brother, said to Him, 'There is a lad here who has five barley loaves and two small fish, but what are they among so many?'

Then Jesus said, 'Make the people sit down.' Now there was much grass in the place. So the men sat down, in number about five thousand.

And Jesus took the loaves, and when He had given thanks He distributed them to the disciples, and the disciples to those sitting down; and likewise of the fish, as much as they wanted.

So when they were filled, He said to His disciples, 'Gather up the fragments that remain, so that nothing is lost.'

Therefore they gathered them up, and filled twelve baskets with the fragments of the five barley loaves which were left over by those who had eaten."

~John 6:5-13

Reflect on this miracle for just one moment.

When God led me to this passage of Scripture, I was stunned by how He used a boy with five loaves of bread and two small fish to do something so amazing.

I felt a little bit like that boy.

I can imagine he must have been a little bit confused. *Surely Jesus can't feed over 5,000 people with my little lunch.* Maybe that little boy even wondered if he should show Jesus the lunch. Maybe his thoughts echoed those of Andrew's, "What could this do amid such a need?"

I too wondered what giving up chocolate tainted by slave labor could do amidst such a desperate need. *Surely God couldn't end slavery in chocolate because people stopped eating it.*

But what did He do with five little loaves and two small fish?

*He fed 5,000.*

It doesn't matter how small your offering, your gift, may be. What matters is that you give it.

And once you begin doing what God tells you to do, you need to take the dare to stand your ground and never back down.

My point in telling you the story of how I gave up chocolate is to show you that not everyone will agree with your dream, or agree with what you are doing to change the world. Not everyone will support you and I can almost guarantee you that you will face opposition.

It's not really a matter of whether or not you can avoid the criticism and opposition, but rather how you will respond.

Jesus guaranteed that we would have to face those who tell us that we aren't making any difference. He told us that we would face those who hate us and want to destroy us. As a follower of Christ this is a guarantee.

*"I have given them Your Word; and the world has hated them because they are not of the world, just as I am not of the world."*

*~John 17:14*

*"If the world hates you, you know that it hated Me before it hated you. If you were of the world, the world would love its own. Yet because you are not of the world, but I chose you out of the world, therefore the world hates you. Remember the word that I said to you, 'A servant is not greater than his master.' If they persecuted Me, they will also persecute you. If they kept My Word, they will keep yours also."*

*~John 15:18-20*

*"Do not marvel, my brethren, if the world hates you."*

*~1 John 3:13*

People in the world will try to stop you from making a difference. They will try to delay your dreams and maybe even criticize and ridicule you.

I have had quite a few people in my life tell me that giving up chocolate is not making a difference in the world. I have had people tell me that they don't think I'll make it in Africa (I mean, hello, there are bugs...).

If you are a teenager, especially if you are a senior in high school, you will be asked quite frequently the question, "What do you want to do with your life? What are you going to college for?"

I would usually respond to this question with the answer, "I'm going to Uganda as a missionary."

Silence.

"Oh, okay, that's nice, but I'm sure you'll change your mind before you grow up," was the usual response.

Or I would give the answer of, "I want to be a lawyer and work in...Africa."

Before the word, *Africa*, left my mouth, most people would respond enthusiastically with, "That's wonderful! Wait...did you say Africa?"

It could be sort of comical at times to see the responses I'd get, but those were the two most common.

To be honest, I wanted to give up. The thought never did cross my mind to go back to eating slavery-tainted chocolate, but there was a time when I thought that maybe I could get away with not going to Uganda.

*Yes, Lord, I know you called me to Africa and I love that place, but could we maybe reach a little compromise? Maybe I could fight slavery here instead of there? Or maybe I could just go short-term and that would be enough?*

But it's when we try to form a compromise that our dreams get pushed to the back burner and our light that was changing the world, slowly begins to burn out.

When God places a dream in our hearts we are usually really fired up about it at the time. It is all that consumes our thoughts and we do whatever we can to make it come true. Trust me on this. I know what I'm talking about.

I used to read countless books on making a difference in the world and showing God's love to others. As soon as the book ended I was so excited about going out and changing the world. However, that feeling only lasted for about a couple weeks until I was faced with my first critic or opposition.

I can almost guarantee that you will feel the same way when you are done with this book. You will be excited about changing your world until...

And that's where the compromise begins.

You look a little different from the rest of the world because you're doing something to bring glory to the Name of Jesus Christ. You are changing your world and making a difference instead of doing what "normal" teenagers do.

So your friends begin to wonder what happened to you. Well-meaning adults encourage you to do something more normal with your life. Parents, siblings, friends, teachers, strangers. The opposition can come from anywhere.

I have been blessed with a family that supports me, even though they'd rather me not pack up and leave for Africa. They still believe in me. I also have amazing friends who encourage me to chase my dreams and make a difference in the world.

But that doesn't mean that others haven't discouraged me. All it takes is one person to try to shut us up and put out our light.

And then we begin to wonder if this is worth it.

We begin the struggle inside of ourselves. We ask God if there is some way that maybe we could go about our dream a little bit differently than we know He is calling us to go about it. We beg Him to send someone else, call someone else. We debate that maybe we aren't that qualified for this job of making a difference and changing the world.

We back down.

We let go of the fire that once burned in our hearts and we step back. We compromise in a little way and it leads to more areas where we compromise.

If we let this happen, we are hindering our efforts to shine God's light in the world and we are settling for something that is less than God's best.

Maybe by calling you to do something completely crazy and irrational in the world's eyes, God is planning for you to change the world in big and mighty ways that only He could have orchestrated. But if you don't follow Him with all of your heart and stand firm in what He has called you to do, you will miss out on all of that. Yes, you may be able to make a difference, but maybe it won't be as big of a difference as what God had in mind. His ways are always perfect, even if they make no sense to you or anyone else in your circle of friends.

Before I continue, I want to make something clear. I am not saying that anytime someone opposes you or gives you constructive criticism, they are trying to turn you away from God's will for your life.

I think I mentioned before that God doesn't use billboards to tell us what He wants us to do, so to know His will for our lives we need to stay close to Him and study our Bibles. However, it is also important to get advice and encouragement from our parents, pastors, and other godly people in your life.

I don't think it's necessary to go to every one of your friends and ask for their advice. You will probably get a variety of responses that will only confuse you more. If you create a group of trusted people in your life that you can go to and share your world-changing ideas with, you will probably have better counsel given to you.

These people still may give you advice that is contrary to what God has specifically called you to do, and if that is the case, then you need to pray hard and continue to follow His leading on your life.

However, if you are not an adult yet, you are still under your parents' guidance and instruction. If they say no to a certain project you want to work on, I am *not* telling you to start a rebellion and stand your ground about what you want to do. If your parents are not believers and they are asking you to do something deliberately against the Bible, that's a different story.

I think it's important to be open and honest with your parents about your dreams and what you feel God has called you to do. When God first called me to Africa, my mom was not going to let me fly half-way across the world at eleven years old. I believe that this was not God saying that He didn't call me. I believe that He was just encouraging me to wait on His perfect timing and, in the process, learn some patience (a quality that I am very much lacking in).

If your parents do not feel that a certain project you want to work on is good for you at this point in time, it doesn't always mean that God isn't calling you to accomplish that task. It might just mean that He isn't calling you to it right now. He more than likely is calling you to wait on His perfect timing. The important thing is that you respect your parents' decision, which is what God is calling you to do right now at this age, and then maybe pursue another dream or goal that He has placed on your heart that your parents agree with you on.

With that being said, the purpose of this chapter is to encourage you to follow God's leading on your life, no matter how many people stand against you in your dream. No matter how many people think that it won't happen, if God has called you to this, then you can know that if you stand firm in Him it will come to pass. Maybe not right now, maybe not in the way you imagined, but it will come to pass one day.

There are many places in the Bible where we are told to stand firm and stand our ground. Here are some of my favorites:

*"Therefore, my beloved brethren, be steadfast, immovable, always abounding in the work of the Lord, knowing that your labor is not in vain in the Lord."*

*~1 Corinthians 15:58*

*"Therefore take up the whole armor of God, that you may be able to withstand in the evil day, and having done all, to stand."*

*~Ephesians 6:13*

Sometimes people won't just discourage you or oppose you in your dream. Sometimes they will oppose your Christian faith and beliefs. When this happens it is vital that you *must* stand firm and hold your ground. It is important that you do not allow them to make you compromise in the area of your faith in Jesus.

When the world attacks our dreams and our longing to change the world for Jesus Christ, we need to realize that if we compromise in this area, we will be more likely to compromise in other areas.

Eventually if we give up on the things that God has called us to do altogether, we will be stumbling in our walk with Jesus because we are not obeying Him. This can lead to turning from Him and compromising on the beliefs that are important and vital to our Christian faith.

So more than anything else I want to dare you to stand firm in your faith.

Yes, sometimes you will stand alone.

Following Jesus and His dream for your life often involves the sacrifice of many things. We will have to stand alone and we will have to be strong.

But even if it feels like you are the only one who cares about the things that God has placed on your heart, and even if it feels like you are the only one standing for Jesus, you need to know that you are not the only one. Maybe there aren't many people around you who share your beliefs or dreams of changing the world in the name of Jesus Christ, but that doesn't mean that there isn't someone just like you out in the world somewhere.

Realizing that there are others standing alone throughout the world somehow makes it easier to remain firm in our faith.

And so, whatever opposition you have faced and however many people have stood against you, I want you to know something.

I believe in you and I believe in what God is calling you to do to change your world.

I believe that if we let Him lead us in life and we follow His calling, we can truly change the world, even if just for one person. But we can't let other people stop us and we can't let other people put out our lights that are shining for Him.

So I dare you to believe in what God is calling you to do.

Be steadfast.

Be immovable.

Stand fast.

*I dare you to never back down.*

## The Fire Within

### A Story...

*Seventeen-year-old Carissa Wilson* stared straight ahead, her brow furrowing over her emerald eyes. A frown formed over her lips and she quickly resisted the urge to raise her hand and her voice. At that moment, the bell rang signaling the end of another long school day.

With a sigh of relief, she jumped out of her seat and joined the rush of seniors heading for the door. The crowded hallway was loud as teenagers talked, girls gossiped in groups and locker doors slammed.

Carissa felt isolated from it all as she tried to make her way out the door without getting caught up in the drama of her high school. Her thoughts were troubled with guilt as she wondered why she didn't raise her hand and speak up that day.

"Carissa! Wait for me!"

The excited voice sounded out of breath as it shouted above the chaotic noise surrounding her.

She slowed her fast pace as she stepped into the bright sunlight, letting it warm her face and wash away her troubles.

Turning with a weak smile, she stretched out her arms to hug her best friend, Maria Thomas.

Maria leaned over and tried to catch her breath. Standing up straight, a mischievous twinkle could be seen in her sapphire eyes. Her raven black hair hung over her shoulder, a sharp contrast to Carissa's light blonde hair.

"Well, we're out of school for the day, *finally*! What do you want to do?" Maria asked quickly, her excited words coming in a rush.

Carissa sighed. "You *do* realize that it's only Monday, right? Never mind, I don't care what we do. Did that science lesson frustrate you?"

Maria cocked one of her eyebrows. "What do you mean? I didn't even really pay attention."

Carissa rolled her eyes and grinned. "That's what I thought you'd say," she laughed with her friend before growing serious again. "It was all about evolution, the 'big bang' theory and all that junk. Has everyone forgotten the Biblical account of Creation?" With frustration mounting in her voice, she added, "I mean, everything at this school is going downhill! All they teach is evolution, everything is anti-Christian and last

166

year they even tried to tell us that we can't bring Bibles! It just doesn't seem fair or right."

Maria shrugged and placed her hand on her best friend's shoulder, "So what? There isn't anything we can do about it anyway, so there's no use in getting all fired up about it."

With a frown, Carissa turned away. "There has to be *something* I can do to bring even just a little bit of God back into this school..." Her voice trailed off in contemplation.

"Good luck," Maria sighed. "I think you just need to let it go. Now, come on. I'll drive." She swung her keys and began to head towards the car.

Carissa fought back the warm tears that stung her eyes. *Why didn't my own best friend even support me?* She shook her head firmly. All she knew was that she *was* going to do something, no matter how many people told her it couldn't be done.

~~~~~~~

With a little excitement in her step, Carissa rushed into school early the following morning.

Her heart was beating just a little bit faster as she hurried ahead of the crowd into the principal's office. Taking a deep breath, she remembered what her mother had told her the previous evening.

*"Just make sure you stand firm in your faith, no matter who stands against you. This isn't going to be easy, dear, but I believe you can do it. Give the glory to God and don't back down from what you believe. You'll do fine."*

Smiling broadly, she faced her principal, Mr. Evans.

He glanced up at her from behind his wire-rimmed glasses and smiled warmly. "Well, good morning, Carissa. I don't remember you doing anything wrong that would require me to see you." He winked at her, knowing that she never got in trouble.

Carissa laughed. "No, sir, I actually came to ask you a question."

"Go for it, Carissa."

She took a deep breath and sent up a silent prayer for support and strength. "I had an idea that needs your permission, Mr. Evans. I would like to start a prayer group here before school starts every morning. I think it would be good for the students to participate in this." She ran out of words to say and held her breath as she waited for his response.

Mr. Evans sighed and rubbed his temples. "Carissa, we are not a *Christian* school," he began and her heart dropped. "But I don't know what I think of this. I mean, I don't see an *issue* with it, as long as it doesn't conflict with school hours. And I also don't want it within the school building. You are free to use the steps outside the school or the parking lot though."

Carissa paused for a moment. "So I can do it?"

"If you must," he sighed.

A grin quickly spread over Carissa's face. "Thank you so much, Mr. Evans! This means so much to me and I know you won't regret your decision to let me do this!" She thanked her principal again before turning to leave and go find Maria to share the good news with her.

"Carissa, you can start this group," Mr. Evans called after her, "But I don't think it will go anywhere. As I said this is not a Christian school and I can't see students supporting you in this. You will more than likely be ridiculed by your peers and made fun of. If you wish to avoid this embarrassment, I suggest you forfeit the idea and choose to do something else. Maybe you could start a chess club or something of the sort?"

Carissa's face fell. "No, sir, this is what I feel God wants me to do. I don't care who ridicules me. I'm not doing it for them. I'm doing it for Jesus."

Mr. Evans shrugged. "Okay, but don't come crying to me when no one shows up."

Swallowing hard against the lump in her throat, Carissa turned and walked out into the chaotic hallway that hadn't changed much since the previous day. She sighed and headed for class, her heart heavy.

*Lord, You wanted me to do this for You. If You want it to happen, please let people show up! And please don't let many people stand against me...*

~~~~~~~

"Hey, what are you doing?"

Carissa turned around and smiled at her friend. "Hey, Maria! I'm hanging flyers for a prayer group that I'm starting tomorrow here at school. I'm really excited about it!" She handed one of the yellow papers to the girl standing at her side.

Maria glanced over it and sighed. "Why are you doing this, Carissa?"

Carissa felt confused. "What do you mean? I'm doing it because it's what God would want me to do."

"Well, count me out. No one is going to go for this. They are going to laugh and call you crazy. It's not worth it. Please, don't do it, Carissa."

169

Carissa was stunned by what her friend was saying. "So you are going to disappoint God because you don't want to risk your popularity?" she asked, annoyance painting her tone.

Maria sighed. "Whatever. Bye, Carissa." With that, she turned on her heel and headed down the hall without looking back.

Carissa's heart felt heavy as she continued to hang the flyers. She fought back the biting tears that stung her eyes.

*Why did she have to act that way?* She thought as the pain of her friend's words continued to sting her heart. *It's just not fair.*

In the pit of her stomach she knew that it was going to be a long day.

"And a long week," she muttered under her breath as she hurried off to her first class of the day.

She managed to avoid Maria most of the day and kept her eyes focused on the floor beneath her during lunch. It didn't take super hearing to overhear the comments and snickering pointed in her direction by anyone who saw the flyers she had hung that morning.

By the time school let out, she ran out the door, her heart pounding and her eyes glassy with unshed tears.

"Mom! Mom, where are you?" she called sadly as she rushed into her kitchen at home.

Looking up from the sink, an older woman smiled and extended her wrinkled hand out.

"Your mother went shopping, dear. What's wrong?" she asked sweetly.

Carissa sighed as she tossed her backpack onto the kitchen counter. "Hey, Grandma. Everything is wrong.

This whole day has been awful!" she replied as a fresh burst of tears overflowed onto her flushed cheeks.

Grandma Wilson nodded her head in understanding. Quietly, she sat down next to her granddaughter.

"Would you like to tell me what's going on?" she asked softly.

Carissa shrugged. "Sure, but I'm not sure what you can do about it." She lifted her tear-filled eyes and choked back her sobs. "My school is all about anti-Christian this and anti-Christian that. It only seems to be going downhill. So I felt as if God wanted me to start a prayer group that meets before school starts out on the steps outside the school. My principal actually agreed so I started hanging flyers today about it, because I want to start it tomorrow. My best friend asked me not to do it and she told me that she wouldn't participate because everyone would make fun of me. Well, she was right. All day at school people would laugh at me behind my back and say mean things. I don't even know if I want to do the prayer group anymore!" She finished with a fresh burst of sobs.

Grandma Wilson was silent as she contemplated how to reply to her distraught granddaughter. "Didn't God call you to this?"

Carissa hesitated. "Well, I guess, yeah. But couldn't I do a little compromise? I mean, I can still do the prayer group, maybe just not at school every morning. I could do it at church on Saturdays," she suggested with a glimmer of hope.

"Is that what God told you to do?"

She sighed and turned her eyes downward. "No."

Grandma Wilson nodded. "That's what I thought. Carissa, listen to me. God never promised that when we followed His will it would be easy. He never promised that people would support us or even like us. He actually even warned us that people would hate us for following Him and doing what He has called us to do in life. The only choice you have to make is whether or not you are going to let that stop you."

Carissa seemed puzzled. "What do you mean, Grandma?"

"You have the choice to give in to the pressure of your peers and stop your prayer group. God isn't going to force you to go through with it. You might miss out on the amazing adventure He has for you, but it's all your choice. If you want to be accepted by everyone at your school, you can back down and quit. But if you want to show your school what you believe and show Jesus how much more He means to you, then you can't back down. Carissa, there is a fire burning within you that is just waiting to shine for all the world to see. If you put out this fire for God, and you give up, then you won't be ready when He asks for something more of you."

Carissa looked thoughtful for a moment. With more tears in her eyes and a smile on her ruby lips, she looked up at her grandmother. "Thank you, Grandma. That means a lot. Jesus is the One that I want to make proud. I want to live for Him and let my fire burn brightly—my fire within."

Grandma Wilson smiled back. "That's my girl."

~~~~~~~

Early the following week, Carissa sat on the steps where she had been assigned to have her prayer group. With a sigh she continued to glance at her watch.

"Well, Lord, I guess it's just You and I...again," she whispered under her breath as she closed her eyes. *I've been sitting here every morning for four days and not one person has come by. Unless you count the people who come to make fun on their way into the school.* She sighed again. *I don't want to give up, Jesus. Please, help me stand my ground and do this for you. Let me shine my light for all to see.*

Smiling, she opened her eyes and jumped in surprise, startled to see someone standing in front of her.

"Hey," Maria whispered softly, her eyes fixed on the cracks in the sidewalk beneath her feet.

"Hi," Carissa whispered back, barely daring to speak.

There was a moment of silence before Maria spoke again. "I've seen you here the past couple days. I just wanted to say that I'm proud of you for doing this. I'm proud of you for standing firm and not backing down, even when we all stood against you. You did the right thing."

Carissa couldn't help but smile at her best friend. "Thank you, Maria. That means a lot. Friends again?"

Maria grinned. "If I can join your prayer group."

Carissa laughed. "Two are better than one!" She patted the seat beside her and took her friend's hand.

"Before we pray, I want to say thank you for coming," she added. "My grandma told me that even if no one else shows up, we are still making God proud. We have His fire and light burning within our hearts and we are letting that shine."

Maria nodded thoughtfully. "The fire within. I like that."

Carissa smiled. "Exactly." Her heart was full of gratitude that her friend had showed up and they could stand for Jesus together.

173

The girls exchanged hugs before joining hands to pray.

~~~~~~~

*"Watch, stand fast in the faith, be brave, be strong."*

*~1 Corinthians 16:13~*

# Chapter Ten

*I Dare You to Open Your Eyes...*

# Chapter 10:
## I Dare You to Open Your Eyes

*Rain pounds the red dirt ground as mud flows in the streets.*

*Dark storm clouds roll across the menacing sky that rumbles with distant thunder.*

*Under a blue tarp that is tattered and dripping, two children sit hunched over.*

*The youngest, barely four years old, shivers as her hollow eyes stare out at the dreary scenery, mud covering her frail body.*

*The oldest, only ten years old, pulls her sister closer to her chest, her own body shivering under the damp tarp. For one so young, she acted as the mother, getting food whenever she could for her little sister. Their bones could easily be seen under their dirty, muddy clothes that hung off their bodies.*

*The oldest girl worried about what she would do next, where their next meal would come from, and how they would survive the cold rain that pelted them with the full force of Africa's rainy season. In her hollow eyes, fear flashed and the pain of heartbreak caused a silent tear to slip from the corner of her eye...*

The heart-wrenching fact is that this is not a story.

Everywhere children are living on the streets without their parents, families are starving, fathers are losing their jobs, babies are being killed, and girls are being sold into slavery.

When I think about the many problems facing our world, I begin to feel overwhelmed. As the statistics fill my ears, I just want to turn away from it all and pretend it doesn't exist.

It is easier to turn and walk away. It is easier to push the images into the farthest corners of our minds, never to think about them again.

Suicide, eating disorders, families torn apart, school shootings, outcasts, bullying.

The list never ends and neither does the need.

People are out there crying out for help and yet, many times, help doesn't come.

I believe that there is a yearning in this generation to stand up and make a difference. I believe that there is a longing in the hearts of young people to change the world and help those who need it.

But when we are faced with the problems and statistics, we feel overwhelmed and choose instead to close our eyes.

Now is the time to open your eyes.

In fact, *I dare you* to open them.

It is our calling to speak up for those who can't speak up for themselves (Proverbs 31:8-9). It is our calling to feed the hungry and clothe the poor (Isaiah 58:7). It is our calling to defend the fatherless and plead for the widow (Isaiah 1:17). It is our calling to set the oppressed free and seek justice for them (Isaiah 58:6)!

Yet how we go about fulfilling that calling looks different for each one of us.

That is usually where the confusion sets in. We are constantly being pulled in every direction to do something about every need surrounding us. We can end up following someone else's calling and ignore our own, because it's easier to be like someone else. It's too hard to step out on our own and risk being different because we have a different passion or dream.

In the next chapter, I want to help you find your calling and discover your passion, but for now, I want to discuss some of the things going wrong in our world. When we hear about certain needs, our heart can break. If that happens, you are probably on your way to discovering your passion.

Discovering my passion started when I read a book about modern-day slavery. But when I think about it, I realize that my dream to end this crime started years ago when God first placed it in my heart.

Obviously I can't talk about everything that is wrong in the world today in the next several pages. So if you don't feel specifically broken over any of the problems I'm going to talk about, don't give up! You can research on your own about something that speaks directly to you.

The first issue that I knew I had to talk about is my very own passion. It is something very close to my heart and something that I believe can be abolished once again.

## *Slavery*

27 million.

What comes to your mind when you hear that number?

Maybe it's the amount of money you'd like to have someday, or the number of Facebook friends you'd like to have (hate to break it to you, but that's probably not going to happen).

When I hear this number my heart breaks.

When I hear this number I imagine a little girl hiding in the dark corners of a brothel. I can see her eyes glistening with unshed tears as she wonders if she'll ever be rescued from the abuse that she suffers every night under the dark sky.

I imagine a little boy with tears on his cheeks as he runs across the battlegrounds of Central Africa. His hand is heavy with the gun he holds and his heart beats faster at the thought of what he'll be forced to do with that weapon. I can see the fear written on his face and in the shadows of his eyes.

I imagine the family trapped in a brick kiln or rice mill with no way out. I can see the sweat pouring down the face of a father who can only look at his young children and pray that they will have a better life than he had.

I imagine the estimated *27 million* people in slavery around the world.[2]

Yes, slavery *still* exists.

We are not all free.

Maybe you are just hearing about this for the first time. Maybe you have heard the words "human trafficking" before but never really thought anything of it. Or maybe you, like me, were heartbroken when you first heard about human trafficking which is modern-day slavery.

27 million is the widely used estimate for the number of slaves in the world; however, it is impossible to know the exact number of slaves in the world and some estimates reach even higher. These are numbers that sometimes we can't even wrap our minds around, but these aren't just statistics.

These are *real* people, just like you and me.

Slavery and human trafficking are not issues that most people bring up in everyday conversation.

But that doesn't change the fact that it exists.

For the millions of slaves in the world, they don't have the privilege of freedom, like we do. They don't have the freedom to choose what they want to eat, or even if they get to eat. They don't have the freedom to decide what days to work, because their trafficker does that for them. They can't even speak out and defend themselves. The most basic of freedoms are stripped away from slaves.

Slavery, or human trafficking as it is commonly called, exists in so many different forms in our world today.

If at any point in time, you thought that slavery or trafficking was not a problem in America, you need to think again. An estimated 14,500-17,500 people are trafficked into the United States annually.

In the United States some common forms of human trafficking/slavery include forced prostitution, agriculture, industry and manufacturing, retail businesses (such as restaurants, nail salons, magazine-sales crews), and private homes (domestic servitude).[3]

Slavery could be in your backyard.

I was heartbroken when I found out that there were some suspected human trafficking locations in cities very close to where I live now. I've been to those cities several times. It was hard for me to even imagine that, as I drove around that city shopping and visiting friends, people just like me could be held by the grip of modern-day slavery.

Do you live in Atlanta, Las Vegas, Orlando or Houston? Large cities such as these are big locations for human trafficking. Even if you don't live in one of those cities, human trafficking could still being going on all around you.

Although slavery is illegal everywhere, it still happens all over the world. In countries like Cambodia, India, Nepal and Thailand, slavery thrives. Throughout the world, every 30 seconds someone becomes another victim of human trafficking.[4]

In these countries and so many others, the illegal sex slave trade operates undercover. Girls, and even boys, are bought and sold into forced prostitution and brothels. Their innocence is ripped away from them and their lives are destroyed, many never making it out of that nightmare alive.

All over the world there are men, women, children and whole families in labor slavery. They are often fooled by the lie of a better life and instead they end up as slaves. Some are forced into bonded labor because of a debt, but as generations go by, the debt never gets paid and the family is stuck in slavery.

It is estimated that there are about 300,000 children forced onto battlegrounds around the world as child soldiers.[5] In Africa children have been used as soldiers for years. They are abducted from their homes and families. Instead of being children, they are forced to murder. Their childhood is stripped away from them in a matter of minutes.

In the Democratic Republic of the Congo, and other countries in Africa, children are forced to work for long hours in awful, dangerous conditions, to give us the minerals and products that make up our smart phones and other electronics.[6]

Do you have a smart phone or laptop or other electronic? If so, there may be child slave labor put into that product. In this age of electronics and media, I think it is important—actually *necessary*—for us to speak up about where our electronics are coming from. We have the power to speak out against this and contact the brands who sell these products, asking them to do something about where they get the materials to make the products.[7]

And for those of you who would probably be ready to either throw this book away or have a heart attack if I told you to give up your phone or computer for a little while, I have a dare for you. No, I'm not telling you to give them up completely.

*I dare you* to put away your phone, iPod, laptop and other electronics, for *30* whole days.

During that time I want you to contact the brands of electronics that you buy from and ask them what they are doing to end slavery in their supply chains. I also want you to get your friends and family to sponsor you to do this, and then give the money you raise to organizations working to fight human trafficking and the use of children as slaves.

Trust me, I don't think a month without your electronics will kill you and, who knows, you might make your parents happy.

After you have put away your smart phone, I want you to take a look in your pantry and refrigerator. Do you see chocolate anywhere in those places?

How about chocolate chip cookies, triple chocolate fudge ice cream, or crunchy chocolate bars that you hide where no one else can find them? Just so you know I *love* chocolate. I guess I used to be what you would call a chocolate lover and I probably ate too much of it. (I know there are those of you reading this who can relate, and I'm proud of you for admitting it.)

But if you read the previous chapters, you are probably expecting what I'm going to say next.

I found out about slavery that exists in the product chain of much of the chocolate that we consume. While we are feeding our "chocolate fix," there are children who are suffering to harvest those cocoa beans. Adults who are not paid properly work long hours to harvest that chocolate. Children work hard and lose out on their childhoods, many having little or nothing to eat.[8]

I knew that modern-day slaves are the ones to give us most of the products that we have in our homes (to do a little experiment, go to www.slaveryfootprint.org and see how many slaves work for you). I knew it existed in our food, clothing, carpets, etc. I also knew that it was probably impossible for me to go 100% fair trade with everything in my home, closet and refrigerator.

So I decided to do the one thing I knew that I could do.

I gave up chocolate.

No, it was not easy at first. It was hard those days when I saw the triple chocolate fudge ice cream in the freezer and I couldn't eat any of it.

But I knew that I wasn't doing this for myself. I was doing this for children I cared about half-way around the world. I was doing it for the sake of freedom and justice for all.

And since the day that I gave up chocolate, God has given me the chance to eat fair trade chocolate. Cocoa that is fairly traded is a lot easier to find now and it makes me very proud of the companies who choose this route. Fair trade companies like Divine Chocolate[9] probably have the best chocolate that you will ever eat in your life. Ben and Jerry's ice cream[10] also sells fair trade chocolate and vanilla ice creams that are really good! Not only does this chocolate taste better, but it is also supporting a fair pay and life for those harvesting the cocoa. I couldn't be more proud to support great companies like these and many others who sell fair trade products.

Slavery is such a big issue and I obviously have not covered everything about it in these short pages. There are so many people trafficked and sold into modern-day slavery every day that it can be overwhelming.

Sometimes it can seem almost impossible to end.

I mean, 27 million is a big number. How could we ever free that many people? And that's only the estimate...

Slavery in America was ended once, and I believe that it can be ended again. I believe that slavery all over the world can be ended. But we need to work together. God is calling up a new generation of abolitionists to free His people and truly make America the "land of the free."

There are many ways to get involved in the fight against human trafficking and, if you feel God leading you in this direction, get involved.

You could work with many great non-profit organizations out there are on the frontlines of this fight against the heinous evil we call modern-day slavery.

Organizations such as the International Justice Mission, Free the Slaves, Not for Sale campaign, Hope for Justice, Love146, A21 Campaign, Restore International, and so many others, are working to restore freedom to all throughout the world.[11] How will you join them in restoring this freedom?

God calls us to free those that are oppressed. In Isaiah chapter 58 we are told to set the oppressed free! In Isaiah 1:17 it says—"*Learn to do good; seek justice, rebuke the oppressor; defend the fatherless, plead for the widow.*"

God loves justice (Isaiah 61:8)! He is calling up those who love freedom and justice to do something about slavery. He wants to use you in this fight and the process of restoring freedom to the victims.

One of the first things to do as a modern-day abolitionist is to pray. This is the most important thing you could do! Pray for the slaves and victims of human trafficking. Pray for restoration. Pray that God would bring justice to the traffickers and that He would change their hearts. Pray for the safety of the people leading the rescue operations. Pray that God would restore freedom to the entire world and to all His people.

Next, use your voice to speak out! Tell your friends and family. Write to members of congress and your representatives, letting them know how you feel about this issue, and asking what they are doing to make sure that freedom is available to all people. You can also have the opportunity to write to rescued survivors of human trafficking by going to the A21 Campaign website.[12]

Use your time, money, and talent.

Watch for signs of trafficked victims in your city. If you notice anything that looks suspicious take the time to call the National Human Trafficking Hotline—1-888-3737-888 or your local law enforcement team.

Dear readers, you have been given the gift of freedom. Please, don't take it for granted. Cherish it and remember how blessed you are to be free. Then decide how you will answer this question:

*How will you use your freedom?*

# Abortion

From 1973 until 2011, over 53 million lives were ended.[13]

Why?

Because of what we call abortion.

Abortion ends a little life *every 26 seconds*.[14]

Ending abortion is one of my sister's passions and I have been very proud of her as she has used her voice to speak out against this issue that needs a voice. These babies in the womb need a voice because they don't have one.

Abortion became legal in 1973 after the infamous Roe V. Wade debate. The government declared abortion legal, giving the right to destroy innocent lives.

There are about 1.2 million abortions per year. There are 3,288 per day, 137 per hour, and, as I mentioned above, one every 26 seconds.[15]

These statistics symbolize the thousands of innocent lives ended. They symbolize the deaths of thousands of boys and girls who will never get the chance to grow up and make a difference in our world. We will never know whether or not they may have grown up to be the next president or great evangelist.

18 percent of U.S. women getting abortions are teenagers and women in their 20's account for more than half of all abortions.[16]

So many young girls out there are getting pregnant and they often see the only way out as an abortion.

So what could you possibly do to make a difference?

One of the first things that can be done is to teach others about the importance and beauty of purity. Pregnancy crisis centers are sometimes allowed to go into schools and teach about purity, which is something that is vitally important in our schools today.

But you also must realize that you have the opportunity to be an example.

Wearing a purity, "true love waits," ring doesn't do anything unless you actually stand by your convictions when the going gets tough. Be an example to your peers of purity and you might be surprised at who follows your lead. Sometimes our peers are just waiting for someone to step out and be different first. This could be your chance to make a big difference.

We can advocate against abortions all we want, but where are we when the girls and women who are pregnant need us? Where are we when they decide to keep the life inside of them?

We need to be there for them.

We need to be the ones to step up and reach out our hands to help them. Befriend a single mother and help her out with grocery trips or other things that need done.

If you have been gifted in the crafty area, try crocheting or knitting baby clothes or blankets for a local pregnancy crisis center. They are usually always open to accepting things like this and it would be such a special gift for a pregnant or new mother.

There are also many great non-profit organizations out there working to advocate against this crime of abortion. Check out organizations like Rock for Life, Abort73, National Right to Life and Save the Storks.[17]

Before closing, I want to add that I think one of the reasons many women are choosing to abort their babies is because they are being taught that life doesn't matter.

In the public school system and in numerous movies and television shows, young children are bombarded

190

with messages of evolution. We are told that life just happened. We don't have a purpose, we just evolved here from animals.

Well, if we don't have purpose and we weren't created by a loving God, then there would be no reason to cherish life and seek to save it.

But this is a *lie*! A lie that has bombarded the minds of our generation.

We *do* have a purpose, one that is so much bigger than we could ever think to dream or imagine. We didn't just show up.

We were lovingly created by an awesome, wonderful Creator. Just read Psalm 139 and you'll see what I'm talking about. God loves us more than we can even fathom and He placed us here at this time in history for a specific purpose.

We must tell the world this. We must tell others how special their life is and that of their unborn child. We must tell others that they were fearfully and wonderfully made.

Because we know this and because we believe this, we know that life is a gift.

Life is to be treasured and held in the highest regard.

Life begins at conception, so no matter what we are told about the baby in the womb, it doesn't erase the truth that there is a life there.

And life needs to be protected.


## Orphans


When God first called me to Uganda, my heart broke instantly for the children there who I knew were

191

orphaned. I have always ached for the children around the world who have to grow up without a mom and dad to be there for them and protect them. I can't even imagine how awful that must be.

Nonetheless, imagine with me for a moment.

Imagine being a young child, and waking up in the middle of the night. All you see is darkness and you can hear the loud thunder booming outside your window every time a flash of lightning lights up your room. You know that there must be monsters hiding under your bed, but instead of running to your parents' bedroom for protection, you squeeze your eyes shut tight and pull the blankets over your head.

You don't have parents to run to. You have to get through that night on your own.

Because you are an orphan.

This is the reality of millions of children across the world.

They don't have a mom or a dad and even sometimes don't have a home or any food. Often times the older children will take care of the younger children. These children don't get to be kids. They have to grow up way too fast.

There are currently an estimated 153 million children throughout the world who have lost one or both of their parents. HIV/AIDS has orphaned an estimated 17.9 million children, with most of them in Sub-Saharan Africa and Southeast Asia.[18]

There are currently an estimated number of 60 million orphans in Asia, giving this region the largest number of orphans in the world.[19]

There are an estimated 120,000 orphans in America and another 400,000 children live without permanent families.[20]

Maybe you have a heart for orphans worldwide and you long to be able to do something about such a deep issue. If so, then I urge you to check out great organizations like World Vision, Amazima Ministries, Holt International or Compassion International, and consider sponsoring a child.[21] These organizations help not only orphans but they help to fight poverty as well and bring education to those who need it. Besides sponsorship, there are many other ways that these organizations reach out to help orphans and other children in need.

You could also get involved with Hoops of Hope, which is a ministry of World Vision.[22] Through this amazing basketball shoot-a-thon you have the opportunity to raise funds for AIDS orphans in Africa. I have participated in a Hoops of Hope event twice and it is such a wonderful experience to be a part of.

Even if you aren't sure what difference you could possibly make for the millions of orphans in the world, I dare you to just reach out and do *something*.

That just might be God's way of using you to change your world.

## Bullying and Suicide

Suicide, eating disorders, cutting...

When I think of these things, my heart breaks for the ones out there who think that this is their only way out of whatever pain they may be facing.

Looking at this generation today you can easily see the pain in many, and yet, the pain in others is sometimes harder to see.

Sometimes we're guilty of assuming that others are fine because they're acting that way. In today's world, we've all become really good at acting. If you think about it, I know plenty of people who could win an Oscar and they've never even been in a movie.

I look out into my generation and I see girls and guys, who fake a smile outwardly, but inwardly they are hurting and sometimes they take that hurt out on themselves or others.

Bullying exists in public schools, the Internet, sports teams, and sadly...even church. And let's face it, bullying hurts. The cruel remarks of others can cut our hearts deeply and scar us.

When you think of issues like bullying, self-injury, or suicide, it's easy to feel overwhelmed and wonder if there is really anything that we could do at all.

But with all of my heart I honestly believe that we can change the world in this area, one person at a time.

I have noticed that in some churches or Christian circles in America today, there is a judgmental attitude. Some Christians turn their backs on that pregnant teenage girl who has no one, because she shouldn't have gotten in that situation. Some Christians shake their fingers at those who wear clothes that they would never consider appropriate.

Even inside the church you see conflicts and arguments over petty things like music, services, outreaches, etc.

What happened to our witness? What happened to being the hands and feet—the body—of Christ?

As professed Christians, the world is watching us.

They are watching to see if we live like love, or if we turn our backs when someone isn't as "spiritual" as we are.

Everyone makes mistakes and Christians are no different. We will mess up and we will fail.

But what I want to know is if we are brave enough to reach out to others different from us and show them the unconditional love of God in tangible form. I want to know if we believe that Jesus loves everyone equally and that we should too.

As the hands and feet of Jesus Christ, we need to be reaching out to the outcast, the lonely, the sinner (that covers everybody), and the needy.

When you see that hurting girl who maybe dresses a little differently than you do, don't judge her and turn your back. Instead go over to her and talk to her. You might be surprised at what she's going through. You might be what she needs at that moment, and for that one person, you might change their world. I have been guilty of judging others before, but God has taught me that as His children we need to *love* others like He does— not judge them.

I encourage everyone reading this to watch their words. Words have the power of life and death (Proverbs 18:21). One careless word spoken without thinking can hurt someone deeply.

I've always probably talked too much (ask anyone), and I truly regret the times when I spoke before thinking and hurt the feelings of others.

"Sticks and stones may break my bones, but words will never hurt me," is probably the most untrue sentence ever spoken by a human being. Words do hurt

and they hurt deeply. We have the ability and the chance to change the world...just by opening our mouths. The only question is whether or not we will change the world for good or for worse.

To those of you reading this who have been hurt deeply and the pain in your heart cuts deep, I want to talk to you for just a minute. To those who have injured themselves physically or who have wanted to take their own life because they didn't think it was worth the pain they were going through, please listen close.

I wish I could sit down with you and look deep into your eyes as I tell you this, but we can imagine.

You are loved.

You are special.

You are needed on this earth *right now* at this specific time in history *for a purpose*.

You were fearfully and wonderfully made. Look up Psalm 139 to see all that God has to say about you when you were made.

You are beautiful, just the way you are. You don't need to change the way you look. God made you just the way you are.

Your life matters more than you know.

I know life can be tough at times and it can seem like nothing will ever change. I can't promise you that if you believe everything I just told you, your life will magically get better and you will be happy. But I can promise you that if you believe what God says about your life, even in the hard times, you will know that He is by your side as you walk through life. You will have the chance to *choose joy*, even in the midst of pain.

If you have injured yourself or contemplated suicide, please speak to a parent, pastor, or other trusted adults.

Please, turn to God and let Him speak truth into your life. This is so important because your life matters so much. God created you for a specific purpose, and if you're still living—no matter how hard it is—your task isn't complete yet. The world still needs you. So, please, from the bottom of my heart, never, *ever* give up.

There are some great organizations out there who would love to help you if you would like help in moving on from destructive disorders or suicidal thoughts. If you feel that your heart breaks for those who don't know how much they are truly loved, you could partner with these organizations to bring help. Fundraise for them, wear their gear to get the word out, and spread a message of hope.

Here are some of the great organizations out there: National Suicide Prevention Lifeline (1-800-273-8255), The Hopeline (1-800-394-HOPE), and To Write Love on Her Arms.[23]

There are also organizations and outreaches that help students reach out to the outcasts and the lonely in their school. I encourage you, if you feel you would like to work in this area, to research more about this on your own.

## With Eyes Wide Open

Now you are familiar with only a few of the problems facing our world today, and maybe you have researched on your own and found out about other issues that tugged at your heart. Now your eyes are open. You have taken that first step by waking up from your slumber and opening your eyes to the issues facing our world that God wants us to do something about.

Does He need to use us? No, He could change all of this on His own if He wanted to. But He *wants* to use us. He placed us here for this purpose. When He sees us open our eyes—the first step in making a difference in this world—He smiles.

So what comes next?

Well, the first thing you could do is read the next chapter. In the next chapter I want to help you discover your passion and figure out what you want to do about it.

But just because you've heard about issues in the world and you've found one that touches your heart, doesn't mean that you can close your eyes again.

We need to constantly live with our eyes wide open. We can't close them anymore.

It's time to stay awake.

*"Is this not the fast that I have chosen:*
*To loose the bonds of wickedness,*
*To undo the heavy burdens,*
*To let the oppressed go free,*
*And that you break every yoke?"*

*~Isaiah 58:6~*

# Chapter Eleven

*I Dare You to Change Your World...*

# Chapter 11:
## I Dare You to Change Your World

*You have a voice.*

And if you've learned anything from this book so far, you know that no matter what some people may say, you *can* change your world.

You have a specific mission in the world that has only been given to *you*. God designed you specifically for this mission and no one can take your place.

You have been born into this generation for a reason and your life is vital to God's plan. This is your, "for such a time as this."

Like I said before, no, He doesn't need you. So go ahead and breathe that sigh of relief.

*He wants you.*

The world is waiting and watching and they are wondering what your next step will be. Many people probably expect you to turn and run the other way. "Change the world? Are you kidding? I'm too young, too small, too shy, too inexperienced for *that*."

But a hurting world is waiting for someone to give them hope and God has chosen *you* for this specific task.

Exactly what your mission and task is or how you will accomplish it, I don't know. That's up to you to figure out with God and I hope that I can help you along the way in this chapter.

For a long time, I wondered exactly what God had me on this earth for. I wondered about my mission and purpose.

Each one of us has been placed on this earth to bring glory and honor to God's Name and to learn how to know Him more deeply, but I wondered how I was supposed to do that.

My dream had always been to do show jumping on my very own horse, but I knew that I was made for more.

Yet even after God called me to Uganda, I felt as if I didn't know what I would accomplish there or what God's purpose for me was once I went.

But when I read a book about modern-day slavery for the very first time, I was completely outraged and heartbroken.[24] That day I knew something.

I was a modern-day abolitionist.

And God's purpose for my life was to bring freedom and justice to His people with the cry of "abolition."

That day so long ago I discovered my *passion*.

I discovered the one thing that made me righteously angry, the thing that broke my heart. I discovered the one thing that I knew I was meant to dedicate my life to doing something about it.

Now it's *your* turn.

What is that one thing, that one need or issue that tears you apart inside? You know, it's that need you hear about and, every time, you have the stirring feeling in the pit of your stomach that you need to do something about it. It's the thing that breaks your heart and makes your tears flow when you think about it. If you know in your heart what this is, then go ahead and write it out on the lines below:

_____

_____

_____

_____

If you don't know quite yet what to write on those lines, that's perfectly okay. I suggest you get a pencil though, because I'm going to have you writing a lot in the next few pages.

First I want you to think back over the needs in the world that we talked about in the last chapter. If none of them stirred your heart, think about other issues in the world that are on your mind. Your passion is already a part of who you are, you just may not have discovered it yet.

Below I have compiled a list of words and I want you to circle the top five words that you think best describe you and your unique personality. If there aren't words there that you think describe you, feel free to add them at the bottom of the list.

The words I listed aren't the only words to use; they're just some that I came up with. Go ahead and get creative and come up with some of your own if you want to! If there are more than five words here that resonate with your heart, go ahead and circle them. But at the end, try to get it down to five.

Ready?

_Let's go..._

| | | |
|---|---|---|
| Acceptance | Endurance | Love |
| Acting | Faithful | Loyalty |
| Artistic | Follower | Mercy |
| Believing | Forgiveness | Multi-tasking |
| Brave | Freedom | Musician |
| Collaboration | Friendship | Organization |
| Compassion | Giving | Overcoming |
| Confidence | Grace | Patience |
| Creativity | Healing | Peace |
| Danger | Helping | Performing |
| Daring | Hospitality | Perseverance |
| Determination | Imaginative | Planning |
| Diligence | Influence | Protecting |
| Discernment | Inspire | Quiet |
| Dreamer | Joyful | Risk-Taker |
| Empathetic | Justice | Saving |
| Encouraging | Leader | Shelter |

| | | |
|---|---|---|
| Singer | Traveling | _____ |
| Speaker | Trusting | _____ |
| Sports | Truth | _____ |
| Teaching | Writing | _____ |

That was a lot of work, but great job on picking five! If you're anything like me, you are tempted to pick half of them and then decide later which five mean the most to you.

Now that you have picked your words, I want you to get quiet for thirty whole minutes. That's right, no music, cell phones, computers, or TV. Facebook and Twitter can wait for your status updates for thirty minutes.

This is the part where you put this book down and you pick up the best Book in the entire world: the Word of God.

Go grab your Bible now. Remember the five words you picked and the problem in our world today that breaks your heart.

Go to that quiet place where you enjoy your alone time with no distractions. Maybe it's out in the middle of your yard listening to the wind whisper through the trees. Or maybe it's in your room with the lights out and candles lit.

Wherever it may be, make your way there now and plan on staying for thirty minutes. You can grab a snack on your way if you want.

When you get to your special place, I want you to have a conversation with the Maker of your dreams, the Maker of you.

And a special note: a conversation is usually when *two* people do the talking, so make sure to listen.

Express to God *your* dreams for your life and then tell Him how you feel about what *His* dreams for you are. Ask Him to show you how your five words could relate to your passion and your way of doing something about the problem that breaks your heart.

Then listen.

Read your Bible and be quiet, listening for God to speak to you. If you don't hear anything, that's okay too. He may choose to reveal His will to you at a different time.

The one word that I circled that resonated with me the most was probably *writing*. I know that God has given me the gift of writing and so I have used that to bring Him glory and to do something about my passion.

When you have finished your quiet time, come back here because I have more writing for you to do...

Welcome back! Are you ready to get to writing again?

Okay, here is your first writing challenge:

What is the deepest dream of your heart? What is that dream that has been yours since you were little, the dream that you want to pursue more than anything?

_____

_____

_____

_____

What is the dream that you feel God is calling you to pursue? How do you feel about it, even if it's different from the dream you have for your life?

_____

_____

_____

_____

How do you think your passion—the thing that breaks your heart—relates to this dream God is calling you to pursue?

_____

_____

_____

_____

Why do you think that the five words you circled are a part of who you are? Do you think they are a part of you because of the specific passion or dream God placed on your heart and life?

_____

_____

_____

_____

When you put this book down, what task or dream are you going to start pursuing today to make a difference in the world? What are you going to do to change the thing that breaks your heart?

_____

_____

_____

_____

If you have finished answering those questions, and filling in all those blanks, you've come a long way. Great job!

You should now have a deeper vision of what your passion is and what God is calling you to do to change the world.

While it may not always be easy, and it will most certainly cost you something, changing your world for Jesus Christ is what God made you for.

In the next few pages I want to share with you stories about modern-day world changers who are doing something about the passions God placed on their heart. I hope you are encouraged by their stories and that they inspire you to go fulfill your own.

## Sue Morganthal-Parson

What does it look like to change your world?

Well, as I've said before, it looks different for everyone. Not one story will be exactly the same.

And sometimes the small stories that might seem meaningless in the world's eyes often make the biggest difference.

The role of a mother is one of the most special roles that God has placed in this world. Mothers are raising the next generation of world-changers, and because of that they are world-changers themselves.

So, of course, I had to share the story of my mother.

Being a mom is not the easiest job in the world. I'm sure my mother would be the first to admit that, especially when you have *two* screaming babies at the same time. ☺

The love of a mother is something that will stay with you for the rest of your life. Home is where Mom is.

Moms stay up late to help you with homework (unless you're homeschooled like me, and in that case, they stay up late grading your work), and they wake up early to pack your lunch and make you breakfast.

Who was there when you took your first step? Said your first words? Who was the one to hang your first painting on the fridge (and, admit it, you didn't have the greatest talent at three years old)? Yep, that's right: *Mom*.

No one understands your quirks and differences much like a mother. They tend to know you inside and out.

My mother does all of this and so much more. She knows that God's calling on her life is to take care of her home and family, raising the next generation of world-changers.

From a young age she taught us about God and showed us what it means to follow Him.

And though it may look small to the world, don't let anyone make you underestimate the role of a mom. They *are* changing the world, just like my mom.

Even though my mom has a great love for her family and taking care of them, she also has another passion in her heart. Being a single mother for nearly fourteen years, she knows exactly how hard it can be at times. She has a heart for other single mothers and longs to be able to reach out to them and help them. Her goal is to open a house for single mothers, to give them a place where they can come and have a "mom's day." Somewhere they can get a free babysitter and get pampered for a day.

Big differences usually happen in small ways. Thank your mom today. Moms are making a difference—*especially mine.*

## MacKenzie Morganthal

*My next story has got to be about the way my sister pursued one of her passions and helped change the lives of so many kids in Africa. But once again, it is better told by her. Here is her story...*

It was Christmas 2011 and my parents had given me a book titled *Take Your Best Shot,* as a Christmas gift. The book was written by Austin Gutwein and I immediately began to read the book because it looked really interesting.

And that's when I found out about Hoops of Hope.

In 2004, when Austin was nine, he had watched a video about a young girl in Africa who was orphaned because her parents had died of AIDS. Austin knew he wanted to help kids who were orphaned because of this horrible disease, and that's why he started Hoops of Hope. Much like a walk-a-thon, Hoops of Hope was designed to use shooting basketballs in order to raise money for the AIDS orphans in Africa. Austin's first event was a huge success as he shot 2,057 free throws and raised almost $3,000. Now, Hoops of Hope has raised over $3 million for this cause and has provided many life giving necessities to people in Malawi, Kenya, Zambia, and India.

As I continued to read about Austin's story and about how Hoops of Hope got started, I remember thinking about those kids and trying to imagine myself in their shoes. I couldn't imagine how these kids must feel waking up every day and wondering if AIDS/HIV would kill their parents that day. I learned that every 14 seconds, somewhere in the world, a child is orphaned because of AIDS/HIV.[25] That means that every day 6,000 children become orphans. I knew right away that I wanted to be a part of Hoops of Hope, and make a difference for these kids.

So I began to get started on hosting my Hoops of Hope event.

I remember being scared to death because it was the first time I had ever hosted such a large event by myself and I was nervous to think about talking to people about the event. But I was able to get a large team together, and on July 28, 2012, my team (Team Hope) shot over 1,000 free throws. Even though my goal was to raise $500, we were able to raise over $1,000. With that event, we were able to feed about 25 orphans in Africa for a whole year.

The next year, on July 27, 2013, I organized my second Hoops of Hope event. On that day, my team (Hoops4Him) raised around another $1,000 while we shot over 2,000 free throws.

After being a part of Hoops of Hope, I have learned to never let fear stand in the way of making a difference or standing up for what you believe in. If I had let my fear of public speaking stop me from hosting my first event, I would have never been able to experience the joy that comes from making a difference in the life of someone else. (And you can get over your fear—I ended up giving a really long speech about Hoops of Hope right before

213

my event and then spoke again to my church's youth group after the event. And I survived!)

So my advice for you is to step out and move past your fear. You'll be amazed at what a difference your life can make in the lives of others.

Be courageous and go change your world!

~MacKenzie Morganthal~


## Bethany

At first glance, Bethany might look like just a normal girl to some.

But she's not.

What makes Bethany different and special? She is allowing the Lord to use her to change the world. Even though she is only a teenager, she is letting God use her to make a difference. More than that though, she knows that, no matter how small her difference may seem, she is still changing the world...one chocolate bar at a time.

In a world where "selfie" is the new word and lots of people are focused more on themselves than on others, Bethany has chosen to give of herself to help others.

Bethany has a passion for children she doesn't even know who are bound by the chains of slavery.

I met Bethany in 2012 and I couldn't have been more blessed. If you get to know Bethany you will quickly see what an amazing friend she is and what a blessing she is in your life.

Over time, I was able to see her passion develop for the victims of slavery/ human trafficking.

You see, Bethany knew about slavery that existed in Africa and other countries around the world, where traffickers sold children into cocoa fields.

When I talked to Bethany about slavery for the first time, she agreed that it was a terrible thing and she felt so bad for the kids in slavery.

Then Bethany realized that she could do something about this, even if it is a small way. She made the decision that she was going to change her world by doing something for the children in those cocoa fields.

She made the decision to give up eating chocolate unless it was 100% fairly traded.

To see Bethany's passion for this was such an encouragement to many people, and she inspired others that she knew.

Bethany has also expressed to me her desire to do something else about slavery. She wants to post facts about trafficking on Facebook, and she has also said that she would like to work in some way with a safe house for victims of trafficking someday.

The true heroes of this world, the world-changers, are usually not the ones out there drawing attention and glory to themselves for what they are doing. The true heroes — the ones who bring a smile to the face of God — are the ones who do something, even something small and believe that God will change the world with it.

*Just like Bethany.*


## *Hannah Murray*


In the summer of 2010 I met a fourteen-year-old girl who would make a big impact on my life. Not only was her enthusiasm for Jesus Christ and the gospel easy to feel, but her encouragement could also uplift even a deeply hurting heart.

Hannah Murray served with her family as missionaries in Tanzania for several years. While on furlough I had the opportunity to meet her parents and later meet her.

Every time Hannah talked about Africa you could see her love for the people she ministered to and her passion to share with them the love of Jesus.

Even after Hannah returned to America, her passion for the lost and hurting didn't change. She continued to serve on short-term missions trips to Canada where she assisted with a children's Vacation Bible School, and even a ministry trip to her own city.

When I asked Hannah what she would like to do one day with her life, her response was that she would like to help troubled youth. Hannah loves horses and has the dream of one day owning a ranch.

Putting both her dreams together, her goal is to own a ranch one day that she can use to make a difference in the lives of troubled youth.

In her words, "Animals can't talk, which makes them great listeners. A perfect formula with troubled youth."

Her desire has always been to bring glory to God with her life and she desires to help others know His love as well. You can see His love shining through her radiant personality.

Ever since I have known her, Hannah has been a great encourager and listener. If I was bothered by something or just plain discouraged, she had the gift of knowing what Scripture verses to point me to and the right encouraging words.

Because of her huge heart to show others the love of Christ, Hannah is working on starting a local group in her city that assists people who need help.

She also has an amazing talent for writing, especially songs and poems that can really touch your heart.

Hannah is a perfect example of getting out there and doing something about the things that burden your heart and continually bringing glory to the Name of Jesus Christ.

## Now it's Your Turn...

There are so many other stories out there of amazing people who have allowed God to use their lives to change the lives of those around them. There are so many other people who have inspired me and encouraged me with their stories.

And now it's your turn.

Someone may read a story about you one day.

So what do you want it to say?

*"But you are a chosen generation, a royal priesthood, a holy nation, His own special people, that you may proclaim the praises of Him who called you out of darkness into His marvelous light."*

*~1 Peter 2:9~*

# Chapter Twelve

*I Dare You to Leave a Beautiful Legacy...*

# Chapter 12:
## I Dare You to Leave a Beautiful Legacy

*******************************************************************

*******************************************************************

*I'm sure you are dying to know* why I left that previous page blank.

And if that thought didn't even cross your mind, humor me.

In the previous chapter I gave stories of real people I know who found their passion and did something about it.

This chapter is *your* story.

Hearing stories of other world-changers can sometimes make you feel as if you are in a different situation than them, and you couldn't possibly change the world that way.

Well, you're right...sort of.

You are in a different situation and you probably won't be changing the world in the same way that they are.

Because you are *you* and God made your story to be unique, just like you are. And that's a really good thing.

You're changing the world in the specific way that God made you to change the world. Can I just say I'm really proud of you? Being confident in who God made you and what He made you to do is hard work, but with great rewards.

At the end of our lives we will all ask ourselves the question, "What was my legacy?"

What are you going to be remembered for? What are people going to say about you? What will generations to come learn about you from others?

One day, when you go Home to be with Jesus, will you give Him a reason to say, "Well done, good and faithful servant"?

These answers can seem overwhelming at times. Yet it is vital to our future that we ask ourselves these questions *now*, instead of waiting until it's too late.

I think that some of us tend to think that we have a long time to think about what our legacy will be. After all, as a teenager, death seems a long way away. We think that we still have plenty of time.

But the truth is that none of us know exactly how long we will have on this earth. None of us are guaranteed of even tomorrow or the next minute.

So the time to think about our legacy is today.

I have always wanted people to remember me as someone who did something about the injustices in the world and who fought hard for the freedom of others, to the glory of God.

I'm sure that you have your own idea of what you want people to remember you for.

But are you working on leaving that specific legacy today? It's that beautiful sort of legacy that only you could leave on this world.

We have to ask ourselves the questions of whether or not we chose to give Jesus all we had. Did we choose to give our all to the time that we have on this earth, or did we waste it? Did we love with all of our hearts? Did we choose Jesus above everything else?

As I thought of this chapter, I figured that the best way to share my heart about this with you was to write a story. So that's exactly what I did.

Oh, and when you're done reading the story, go back and fill in that blank page. Don't worry about how messy it looks or how unfinished it may be. This is your legacy, no one else's. Fill that page in with the story of *your* life.

# Beautiful Legacy

## A Story...

*"Six months."*

Silence descended upon the white hospital room and tension hung on the air like the icicles that cling to the roof of a house in the winter.

Seventeen-year-old Violet Carter felt her breath catch in her throat. Shock flooded over her and she nervously blinked back the hot tears that burned her emerald eyes.

Slowly she began to pick at a loose string coming from her hospital gown. The clean, lemon scent of the room overwhelmed her at that moment, and she longed to disappear into the white walls that loomed on every side of her.

Swallowing hard, she flipped her long, auburn braid over her shoulder and tried to calm her racing heart.

"There's nothing we can do?" Violet was brought back to the present by the small, worried voice of her mother.

Mrs. Carter stared at the doctor, her face ashen. She reached over quickly to clutch her husband's hands, her knuckles turning white.

"I'm afraid not," Dr. Stephens replied gently, with a look of sympathy entering his eyes. "The only thing that could possibly help would be a kidney transplant, but it's still no guarantee."

"She's only seventeen," Mr. Carter whispered, his voice gruff with emotion. He suddenly seemed to find the white linoleum floor very interesting.

"But couldn't we try a transplant?" Mrs. Carter inquired in a voice that sounded desperate.

Dr. Stephens sighed. "We would try if we could. Her blood type is hard to match and right now there are no possibilities. We have put her on a list, but there are two other patients ahead of her."

Violet clenched her hands and bit her lip until she tasted blood. *They're talking like I'm not even sitting right here,* she thought in frustration.

"So pretty much I'm dying," she finally blurted out, her tone void of emotion. "I've only got six months to live."

Her own words seemed to bring the realization to her that she would never see her eighteenth birthday. Panic began to overwhelm her. *I don't want to die...*

Mrs. Carter jumped up quickly and pulled her daughter into her loving embrace. "Don't worry, honey," she whispered soothingly. "God will work everything out. He'll get you in to have that transplant."

Violet twisted her ruby lips into a frown before looking away from her mother quickly.

She slowly began to tune out all the voices around her as her parents talked things over with the doctor. Her heart began to pound slowly as reality began to sink in again.

*I'm only seventeen. I can't be dying! I'm a teenager and gonna be a senior in high school. I have my whole life ahead of me. Can this be real? Oh, God, where are You? Why are You letting this happen? Please, wake me up. This has to just be a terrible nightmare.*

"Do you want to go get ice cream, Vi?" Mrs. Carter asked her daughter. She placed her arm around Violet's shoulders and pasted on a plastic smile.

Violet had barely even noticed when Dr. Stephens left. As she walked down the hospital hallway with her parents, her mind began to reel. The strong clean smell overwhelmed her again as she stared at the white walls.

Slowly she shook her head. "No, I want to go home."

Mrs. Carter exchanged a quick glance with her husband. Sighing softly, she forced another smile and nodded. "Alright, sweetie, we'll go home."

"We can watch that movie you've wanted to watch," Mr. Carter suggested as he hurried to pull open the glass door for his wife and daughter.

Violet shrugged and tried to smile, if only for the sake of her parents. *Please, don't act so normal,* she wanted to scream.

Time seemed to be in slow motion as the Carters stepped into the California sunshine and headed for their SUV.

Violet took a deep breath and closed her eyes briefly. She had always loved summer. She let the warm rays of the sun soak into her skin before slipping into the backseat of the vehicle.

When her parents got settled, her father looked back at her and reached for her hand.

"Can we pray?" he asked softly.

Violet reluctantly took his hand, but instead of closing her eyes, she let them gaze across the nearly empty parking lot.

"Father, we come to You now asking for healing of our precious little girl, Violet Faith," Mr. Carter began before his voice broke. He cleared his throat before trying again.

As he continued to pray for healing, Violet tuned out his rich, deep voice that had always been a comfort to her. Tears filled her eyes and she felt sobs bubbling up inside of her.

*I won't be here next summer... I won't get to graduate. I won't get to be married. I won't get to have kids. I won't get to make a difference in the world.* Swallowing hard, she let the tears overflow down her flushed cheeks. *I won't get to live. How can this be happening to me?*

"Violet, are you okay?" The words from her mother were gentle as Mrs. Carter stroked her hand slowly.

Violet looked up, tears still streaming down her cheeks. She pushed away her strong façade and wrapped her arms around herself, sobs beginning to shake her shoulders.

"I don't want to die, Mom," she whispered in reply, her words barely audible through the sobs that continued to make her body tremble.

Mr. Carter clenched his jaw to keep his own tears from falling as he stared at his young daughter.

"I don't know why you have to go through this, honey," he whispered, his voice choked by emotion.

"But you don't know what God will do," Mrs. Carter added, trying to be positive. "He could get you a kidney donor or He could heal you completely. You can't give up all hope, Vi."

Violet sighed. "Mom, did you not hear the doctor? I'm dying. God didn't answer our prayers."

Mrs. Carter gasped as tears filled her sapphire eyes. Turning away from her daughter quickly, she silently prayed for the words to say. *God, help us...*

Mr. Carter refused to look his daughter in the eyes. "Sweetheart, God is ultimately the one in control of the situation, not the doctors. He is the only One who knows what is best for all of us. We just need to trust Him right now."

Violet shook her head and leaned back. Closing her eyes, she felt her stomach turn over and she thought she might be sick.

When she opened her eyes again, tears clouded her vision. She didn't know what to do anymore. Nothing made sense to her. The only thing that she knew for certain was that she wanted out of this nightmare. She didn't want to die.

*God, if You are truly there, then do something. Do something soon.*

~~~~~~~

*Two weeks later...*

Violet stared up at the ceiling fan as it spun around in a circle, sending cool air down on her. Tears slowly slipped out of the corners of her eyes and slid down her flushed cheeks. For two weeks she had managed to avoid the questions of her friends when they would call, asking how the doctor appointment went. She didn't want to tell them, not yet. It would hurt too much to have them act differently around her.

But today was the first day of school and the first day of her senior year. There was no way her thoughts were going to focus on chemistry and algebra equations.

"Vi, honey, the bus is going to be here soon! Please, come downstairs," her mother called up the oak staircase, her voice echoing on the hardwood floors.

Violet sighed and slowly got off of her bed. She ran a brush through her hair quickly before glancing at her calendar. Each day she crossed off was another day she was never going to get back. Panic overwhelmed her at the realization that her time truly was running out.

Entering the kitchen, she saw her parents sitting at the table, holding hands. Sensing her presence, they both looked up with forced smiles.

"Sit down, Vi," her father invited. Mr. Carter patted the seat beside him. "Your mother and I were talking about some things."

Violet slowly sat down. "Like what?" she asked curiously.

Mrs. Carter took a deep breath. "Ever since your last doctor's appointment, you have been very distant. I don't blame you. I can't even wrap my mind around this whole situation. I can't imagine life without you." A sob caught in her throat and she broke off her sentence. Violet blinked back her tears as she took her mother's hand and squeezed it.

"But, Vi," Mr. Carter began, "you can't blame God for this. We don't know His reasons for letting you walk through this. We don't know whether you have six months or longer. We don't know what the future holds. No matter what happens, we have to trust Him. You do trust Him, don't you, dear?"

Violet took a deep breath and brushed away her tears. Looking up bravely, she nodded. "It has been hard and at first I was really angry. I felt abandoned by God. But last night I was reading my Bible. I began to wonder something. What are people going to remember about me one day when I'm gone? What will my legacy be?" Her tone turned contemplative. "So instead of using the time I have left to be angry with God, I'm going to trust Him. I'm going to give Him everything I've got and I'm going to make a difference with the time I've got left."

Mrs. Carter had tears streaming down her cheeks as she embraced her only daughter. "We are so proud of you and always know that we are here for you."

"Right now, though, it looks like your bus has finally arrived. Are you sure you want to go today?" Mr. Carter added worriedly.

Violet nodded as she stood and embraced both her parents. "I want to use every day I can to make a difference. Today I'll see who I can reach out to at school." With a smile she waved goodbye before walking out into the early morning sunshine.

For once in her life she was suddenly aware of the influence she had in the world. She was suddenly aware that life was more than what she could do for herself, but instead, what she could do for someone else. No matter how much time she had left, in her heart she was determined to leave a beautiful legacy worth remembering.

~~~~~~~

The excited chatter around the lunch table continued to rise as conversation carried on. Violet glanced around at her friends as they all laughed and joked.

Two of Violet's best friends, Elizabeth and Sara, sat on either side of her, trying to draw her into the conversation and laughter. Yet Violet's thoughts were elsewhere.

"Who's that?" she finally asked softly, directing the question to Elizabeth. Her eyes were fixed on a girl sitting behind them.

Elizabeth glanced behind her and shrugged. "I don't know her name, but earlier Luke was saying that she just moved here. So she must be new. Looks like she doesn't have any friends yet," she added before turning back to her lunch and taking a bite of her lemon crème cookie.

Violet looked thoughtful for a moment before placing a hand on her friend's shoulder. "I'll be right back," she told them all. Sara gave her a quizzical look but didn't ask questions.

Slowly, Violet made her way over to the back table that was the company of only one person. She nervously pulled out one of the blue chairs. "Hi," she greeted slowly. "I'm Violet. What's your name?"

The young girl sitting in front of her lifted her head. "Um, I'm Alyssa," she replied cautiously. "What do you want?"

Violet was caught off guard by her tone. She sat down and shook her head. "I don't want anything. You just looked lonely so I thought I would come over and keep you company."

Alyssa cocked her eyebrows. "Really? You're the first person to actually be nice to me. Everyone else has only come up to tease or make fun." She rolled her eyes angrily.

Violet knowingly nodded her head. "Yeah, high school can be that way sometimes." She laughed. "So did you just move here?"

"Yeah, when my parents divorced. I ended up here with my mom. I came from New York, so California is a big difference." She laughed for the first time.

Violet laughed too. "I bet," she agreed as she continued to ask more questions to get the conversation going.

After a few minutes the lunch bell rang and everyone began to head for the door.

"Alyssa, I decided that I'm going to be doing a Bible study in the library here after school hours. I just talked with the principal about it this morning. Do you think you'd like to come tomorrow?" Violet asked her new friend hopefully.

Alyssa seemed to draw back at the mention of a Bible study. "I don't think so," she replied coldly. "I'm not much into that sort of thing. God forgot about me a long time ago."

Violet thought her heart might break at the familiar words that she herself had wondered only a short time previously. Taking a deep breath, she chose to be bold. "I thought that too not long ago. But the truth is, just because we don't see the whole picture, it doesn't mean that God forgot about us. It just means that He's using us in ways that even we couldn't imagine. Please come tomorrow, Alyssa. Just give it a try."

Her new friend sighed. "I don't know." Looking up quizzically, she asked, "If you don't mind, why did you think God forgot about you?"

Violet held her breath. *Do I tell her? None of my friends know yet. Should I tell her, God?* The nudging in her heart wouldn't go away so, closing her eyes briefly, she replied, "Two weeks ago I found out that I'm dying. I only have six months left to live."

Alyssa gasped, the shock registering on her face. She seemed at a loss for words.

Uncomfortable, Violet quickly waved. "See you tomorrow?" she asked over her shoulder.

"See you tomorrow."

~~~~~~~

*Five months later…*

232

"How have you been doing lately, Vi," Mrs. Carter asked her daughter as she spread some butter on a freshly toasted piece of bread.

Violet's eyes lit up as she leaned against the counter next to her mother. "I'm doing great, Mom!" she responded enthusiastically. "At school, my Bible study has really grown. Fifteen girls are coming, including Liz and Sara. Two of the girls became Christians last week and it was so amazing to be a part of! And at the soup kitchen on Saturdays, there are so many nice people to get to know. I'm having so much fun with all of this!" She put a strawberry in her mouth and laid her head on her mother's shoulder.

Mrs. Carter smiled softly. "You truly are making a difference, my dear. But how is your pain? Last week the doctor said that your pain might get worse now." A trace of fear and anguish passed over her face but she brushed it off for her daughter's sake.

Violet shrugged. "Actually, I don't have much pain at all. I'm feeling great!" She winked. "Maybe God is healing me. You never know."

Mrs. Carter winked back. "He just might be," she agreed. "Now I think I see Alyssa coming up the street, so you better go meet her."

"Thanks, Mom!" Violet replied. Growing somber, she added, "Do you think you could pray for Ally? She seems close to accepting Jesus into her life, but hasn't quite reached that point yet. I know life has been hard for her and I really want her to know the love of her Heavenly Father."

Her mother nodded vigorously. "Of course, Vi. I'll be praying hard."

Violet smiled before rushing out into the sunshine and into her friend's open arms. Pulling back from their hug, she took Alyssa's hands. "I've been feeling a lot better," she enthused. "Maybe God's healing me."

Alyssa grinned at her friend's enthusiasm. "I bet He is." Tears formed in her eyes. "After all, I can't lose you yet."

Violet's chin quivered slightly. Swallowing against the lump in her throat, she nodded. "I don't really want to die yet either, but if I do, I know where I'll be going. And I'll see Jesus!" She smiled and took Alyssa's hand in her own. "Ally, if anything happens to me, promise me that you'll turn *to* Jesus and *not* away from Him. I know you're not completely ready yet, but if I die, promise me you'll at least go to church with my parents."

Alyssa nodded as a tear slipped out of her eye. "Yeah, I promise. I promise with all of my heart. Now let's go! You're feeling great, so enough tears! When we get to the ice cream shop I'm getting a peanut butter sundae."

Violet laughed and linked arms with her friend as they happily discussed their favorite ice cream flavors.

~~~~~~~

Rain slowly dripped from the dark clouds gathering in the sky. The droplets made ripples in the puddles across the paved parking lot.

A lone, girlish figure slowly made her way across the pavement, her eyes downcast. Her dark colored skirt swished around her ankles in the wind. Her emerald eyes held tears in them as she slowly took a deep breath. Lifting her head, she reached out her trembling hand to open the tall, heavy door looming in front of her.

A blast of warm air greeted her the instant she entered the long corridor. A tall gentleman smiled sadly in her direction and handed her a piece of paper.

Willing herself not to cry, she took it and slipped it into her Bible that meant so much to her now. She clutched it close to her chest as she quietly slipped into the back of a crowded room. People stood everywhere and there were no seats to be seen.

At the front of the room, a middle-aged couple stood with their arms around each other as they cried.

Taking in the scene, the young girl felt her breath catch in her throat. *This can't really be... Oh, why'd she have to leave?*

She listened quietly as numerous people took turns holding a microphone and talking about Bible studies and soup kitchens. She smiled at some of the stories and cried at the others.

Finally, a voice called out. "Is there anyone else who would like to say something about the young life we are remembering today, Violet Faith Carter?"

Before she could convince herself otherwise, she quickly raised her hand and began to walk to the front of the crowded room. At the front of the aisle, Mrs. Carter smiled warmly at her before they embraced.

She took a deep breath as tears poured down her cheeks. Her shaking fingers ran over the smooth casket in front of her briefly, before she turned back to the people who waited for her story.

"Hi," she said hoarsely into the microphone. She cleared her throat and tried again. "My name is Alyssa Collins. I'm seventeen years old and I only met Vi a short time ago. Vi was the type of person who could light up a room. When I first met her, I never would've guessed that she was dying. Vi came up to me at lunch on the first day of school. It was an awful day for me. Actually it was an awful day that was part of an even worse week. The day that Vi came up to me, she knew that I was having a rough time and that I was lonely. What she didn't know was that I was going to commit suicide that day."

Tears poured from Alyssa's eyes as she continued her story. "Violet quickly became my best friend. I miss her terribly. The last day I saw her alive, we thought she was getting better. We went for ice cream and she spoke to me about leaving a legacy. It was what she wanted more than anything. She talked about it all the time. I just wanted to say that she did leave that legacy. This room and all these people in it are proof of that. Vi left me her Bible and because of her example of unwavering faith, I decided to accept Jesus into my heart."

Slowly the room began to break into applause, as the tears flowed for the girl who would be deeply missed.

Alyssa handed the microphone back to Mrs. Carter, who embraced her warmly.

"My Vi did leave a legacy, didn't she?" Mrs. Carter whispered through her tears.

Alyssa nodded and smiled as tears continued to pour down her own cheeks. "Yes, Mrs. Carter, she did. She left a beautiful, beautiful legacy."

~~~~~~~

*"I, therefore, the prisoner of the Lord, beseech you to walk worthy of the calling with which you were called."*

*~Ephesians 4:1~*

# Chapter Thirteen

*Who Are You Living For?*

# Chapter 13:
## Who Are You Living For

*If you have found your passion* and you are excitedly living out your dreams, that's great.

But now you have to answer a question that will be vitally important to every area of your passion, dream and, ultimately, your life.

This question is one that cannot be taken lightly.

This is the question that will determine why you have this passion and why you are going about changing the world in the way that you are. It will help clarify for you the motives you have in making a difference. This question could change *your* life.

*Who are you living for?*

## Me

In today's society the word "others" has been replaced with "me" and "mine."

Selfishness is accepted, even praised, especially in teenagers.

Don't believe me?

Well, when was the last time you looked in the mirror just to admire your beautiful hair? The last time you took a "selfie" (don't tell me you don't know what I'm talking about)? The last time you yelled at your brother to give you the basketball because "it was *my* turn"? The last time you turned away from giving your five-dollar bill to a homeless person on the street corner because you were on your way to buy ice cream?

None of these things are exactly wrong. Checking your hair in the mirror isn't wrong—unless you've done it every five minutes for the past two hours and you're starting to feel prideful because you look so cute. (Come on, girls, admit it. We've all done this at some point in time.) Taking a selfie can be fun and isn't wrong—unless you take one multiple times a day and don't feel happy until you do. Telling your brother that it's your turn for something isn't wrong—unless you feel entitled to having it right at that moment and you argue until you get what you want. Passing up the chance to help a homeless person isn't necessarily wrong—unless you know that, in reality, you could probably do without that ice cream cone this time.

There is no denying the fact that we live in a self-absorbed world. There are TV shows, magazines, music, advertisements, etc., that exist for the express purpose of showing us the next thing we must do to be happy.

We need to pamper ourselves more and take more time for ourselves. We need to buy the latest beauty product so that we can be prettier. We need to buy the latest game station so that we can have a better one than our friends.

In all reality, our world tells us: *it's all about me.*

Yet when you live for yourself you will never truly be happy. The world and the TV may tell you that you will be, but you won't. I can promise you that.

You may see celebrities with plastic smiles who look happy on the surface. But if you dig deeper, their lives may tell a different story.

A good way to know whether or not living for yourself is what will truly make you happy is to evaluate it by the Bible. So what does the Bible say about living this way?

*"Let us not become conceited, provoking one another, envying one another."*

~*Galatians 5:26*

*"Then He said to them all, 'If anyone desires to come after Me, let him deny himself, and take up his cross daily, and follow Me. For whoever desires to save his life will lose it, but whoever loses His life for My sake will save it. For what profit is it to a man if he gains the whole world, and is himself destroyed or lost?"*

~*Luke 9:23-25*

When we live for ourselves, we are not taking up our cross daily. When we live for ourselves we are not losing our lives for the sake of Jesus.

Living for ourselves and our own selfish pleasures only leaves us empty on the inside. It only leaves us wondering if there is really more to life. And there is.

Living for ourselves will, in the end, make us unhappy because we were made to give our lives away for Jesus.

If you feel that you are being hindered in your ability to make a difference in the world, examine your heart. Maybe you'll see some areas where you are taking "selfies" outside of the camera.

If you are pursuing your dreams solely for yourself and your own benefit, you may need to evaluate your motives. If you are seeking to change your world only so that you can get credit and the spotlight, it may be time for a heart check.

Pursuing your dreams because it makes you happy and it makes you feel truly alive, isn't wrong. When you are doing the thing that God made you to do, you will feel joy. It only becomes wrong when you pursue your dreams or change your world *only* for yourself. Your goal is not to leave yourself out *completely*, but instead shift the focus to Jesus and keep it on Him, instead of having an "it's all about me" mindset.

If you're anything like me, you can sometimes get tripped up when you switch your focus to others, because slowly you begin to live *for them*.

## Others: Unbelievers

Have you ever found yourself acting a certain way just so that someone else will like you?

We dress a certain way so that we "fit in" with the crowd. We talk a certain way so that people will like us. We act a certain way so that we have more friends.

Some people are just born with the desire to please others. That's not a bad thing. In fact, it can be a pretty good thing. They can be the ones who help maintain peace and create a peaceful environment.

However, some of us can cross the line into *living* for other people or living to please them. There are so many different types of people that we live for, or act as though we are living for, but I just separated them into two categories: Unbelievers and Christians. Yes, often we even live for other Christians, sometimes without knowing it.

Part of this can come from not wanting it to be about us, but instead about others. While it starts out with good motives, we eventually become so consumed with making sure it's not about us, that we end up living for the sole purpose of making others happy.

And sometimes, we live for other people because we are just plain scared. We are scared that they won't like us. We are scared that we won't fit in or be good enough. We are scared that if we are different from them, they will end up not liking us because of that. And so we let our fear drive us into living for them.

First, I want to talk about when we live for unbelievers.

We live for them when we are so afraid of offending them that we don't bring up Jesus at all. I am sometimes guilty of this. And when I find myself wanting them to like me so much, I have to ask myself: Would I rather them not like me or would I rather them die not knowing Jesus?

We live for unbelievers when we want them to accept us so that "we can tell them about Jesus." Even when their acceptance means that we have to compromise our beliefs. Even when their acceptance means that we have to dress in a way that we know we shouldn't, say things that we know aren't right, or act in a way that we know is not godly.

We live for them when we make the decision to do whatever it takes to get their attention, even if it means compromising their eternal destiny.

When we live for them, it has real consequences. Our lives become affected or theirs do.

Please, believe me when I say that I do not think that we have to stay away from unbelievers completely to avoid falling into the trap of living for them. That view, I believe, is wrong in a way. To tell them about Jesus we have to know them. To show them His love, we have to befriend them.

But being their friend doesn't mean that we have to live for them. It doesn't mean that we have to change who we are just so that we can hang out with them. We can still live out our faith.

When you are able to live out your faith and do the right thing around your unbelieving friends, that's when you realize that not living for them is the best thing…for both of you.

## Others: Christians

Oh, how many times I have fallen into this trap of living for other believers, other Christians.

As Christians, we all have one basic foundation: our faith in Jesus Christ. This is what unites us into one family. Yet we all have different views or beliefs on certain subjects. We all have differences and that is only normal, because none of us are exactly the same, and we never will be. It's good to accept the differences of others and love them anyway. There are times though when pleasing everyone and agreeing with everyone is humanly impossible. It's good to try to work through these situations, but sometimes it's better to just part ways, like Paul and Barnabas did (Acts 15:36-41).

Some of us, however (myself included), can get caught up in trying too hard to make others like us, that we begin to live for them. Like I said, this is usually a response to fear.

You know what I'm talking about.

This happens when we bring up certain conversations around certain people because we know that it will make us look more "spiritual" to them. And then we don't bring up those same conversations to others Christians because they have a different view on that subject.

We live for them when we dress a certain way just so that our Christian friends will like us. And then we dress differently when they aren't around.

We live for them when we agree with their point of view on a certain spiritual discussion, even if our view is completely different.

I think you get the point.

Craving the acceptance of other believers so much that we act hypocritical is wrong. What I mean by this is when you believe one thing and you hold that belief around some of your friends, but around other Christians you agree with *their* belief, even if it's different from yours.

Whether you're living for unbelievers or other Christians, both ways of living will leave you feeling utterly exhausted and incomplete. If you live for others because you are afraid of not being accepted, chances are, even if you live for them, you will still struggle with this fear. The only way to release this fear is to live for the only One who can make us complete...

## God

As you have read through the last few pages, have you wondered if you're living for yourself? Or if you've been living for others?

If you've been living for anyone other than Jesus Christ, you are probably feeling incomplete. You may even be feeling torn, hypocritical, or hurt.

That's because living for yourself won't fill you up on the inside. Living to please everyone else won't make your fears go away.

Let me share with you a verse again:

*"Then He said to them all, 'If anyone desires to come after Me, let him deny himself, and take up his cross daily, and follow Me. For whoever desires to save his life will lose it, but whoever loses His life for My sake will save it. For what profit is it to a man if he gains the whole world, and is himself destroyed or lost?"*

~Luke 9:23-25

We need to lose our life.

Not in the same sense that you would lose your keys or your cell phone.

No, we need to give up our life and die.

Hopefully not literally, although in other countries many brave, courageous Christians have died for their faith and belief in God. Still many others face that threat even today.

While this verse in Luke could be talking about dying for Jesus literally, I also believe that it is talking about dying for Him daily.

*Take up your cross daily and follow Him.*

It's about dying to yourself and instead living for Him.

See? We're only supposed to be living for *Him*. No one else, not even ourselves!

When you live truly for Him alone, your life will change. He is the One we were made to live for. When you live for your God alone you will have a freedom that you didn't have before, not to mention a peace.

You won't have to keep striving to make everyone else happy. You won't have to keep striving to make others like you or accept you. You won't have to keep striving to be happy. You won't have to keep striving to be good enough, only to feel exhausted in the end.

Because when you live for Jesus, you are enough in Him. You are already accepted (Romans 15:7), loved (John 3:16), chosen (1 Peter 2:9). When you live for Jesus, He fills you with joy which lasts a lot longer than the emotion of happiness (Psalm 16:11).

Will living for Jesus always be easy? Will it always be popular?

*No!*

But it's worth it.

You may not receive the acceptance of others for living for Him. You may not be popular among some of your friends. You may not always make everyone else happy.

But that's okay.

If you are living for Jesus and doing what He has called you to do, you're doing the right thing.

So live for Him *alone*. Not for yourself. Not for your unbelieving friends at school. Not for your teachers, parents, siblings, youth pastor, or Christian friends.

Only for Him.

Take up your cross and live for Him daily.

That's a dare.

*"For do I now persuade men, or God? Or do I seek to please men? For if I still pleased men, I would not be a bondservant of Christ."*

*~Galatians 1:10~*

# Chapter Fourteen

*Let God Write Your Story*

# Chapter 14:
## Let God Write Your Story

*The title of this chapter pretty much sums up the basic message of this book.*

Once you push past your fear, break away from the lies you've believed, discover your passion, begin to make a difference in this world, and start living for Jesus alone, you are heading in the right direction.

But if you don't let God write your story, all of these other good things will start to fall apart.

I know that sometimes it can be hard to trust God with the pen of your life story. It can seem as if He is writing the wrong chapter or He's taking too long to get to the right one.

I may have mentioned before that I am not the pinnacle of patience. In fact, my patience department runs on zero most of the time (I'm working on it!). I just don't seem to have the patience to wait for anything (which is probably why God sees fit to have me wait for *lots* of things *lots* of the time).

There have been times in my life journey, even now, when I wonder why God is taking so long to bring me to the place where I can finally pursue my dreams. I want to act like a three-year-old, grabbing the pen and switching around a few chapters of my life so that I can do what *I* want *now.*

Since God isn't a drill sergeant, He won't demand that I give Him that pen back. He won't demand that I let

Him finish writing this chapter of my life. As a loving Father, He will sit back and wait for me to get frustrated of doing it on my own, until I finally hand it back to Him.

If you've ever wished that you could start writing your own story—leaving out some parts and changing others—you're not alone. I've been there before and I'm sure many others have too.

We just sometimes think that we can do it better. We think that we can write it better. We think that certain difficult situation in our life would be better left out. We don't understand why God let us get hurt by that person and so we wish we had a backspace button for our life, just like on our computer keypads.

But life doesn't work that way.

And, oh, am I so glad it doesn't.

Yeah, when I'm *in* the situation I wish there was more than just a backspace button. I'm looking for the delete button to get rid of the whole chapter.

But when I look back I realize that God knew what was best all along. I am only human and I couldn't see the whole picture. I still can't.

If that hurtful situation wasn't a part of my story, I wouldn't have grown stronger. If I didn't know those certain people in my life that can drive me crazy, I wouldn't be the person I am today. If I didn't experience that chapter that I wasn't thrilled about at first, I wouldn't have known the joy and beauty that followed the chapter title.

God is the One who created us and made us. He knows us so much better than we know ourselves or anyone else knows us. And He loves us and always wants what is best for us (Jeremiah 29:11; Romans 8:28).

Don't you agree that trusting Him with the pen of your life or with the writing of your next life chapter is so much better than trying to do it on your own? I think so.

So what exactly does it look like to let God write your story?

Well, for one, do what He asks you to do, without hesitation. You may not like it and you may not think it fits this chapter of your life, but trust me, it will. If God is leading you to it He has a perfect plan for it.

So follow Jesus with all of your heart.

Be recklessly, radically dedicated to following, obeying and loving Him no matter what.

Grab that notebook of yours and start to journal about the wonderful adventure God is leading you on. Write down the things He is asking you to do and the joy that comes after you do it.

But if there's one thing I've learned about following Jesus wholeheartedly, it's this:

*Following Jesus wherever He leads you doesn't always mean geographically. Sometimes it means spiritually.*

God may or may not call you to pack up and move to Africa. He may or may not call you to follow Him to a different state.

But He is calling you to follow Him.

Is there someplace spiritually that He is calling you to go, but you've been holding back?

What about that girl at your church or school who makes fun of you and you don't want to forgive her? You don't want to step out spiritually into that scary place of forgiveness and love, even though you know that God is calling you to follow Him there.

What about the dream that you just keep holding onto because you're afraid? You don't want to let go of that hope or dream because you know God might ask you to step out into that scary place of letting it go and pursuing something else instead.

What about the worry that you just don't want to stop? You are afraid that if you trust God with everything, things won't go as you want them to. Even though you know God wants you to step out into that scary place of complete trust in Him. Yet you're still afraid to let Him write your whole story, so you worry.

What about the anger, the harsh words, or the disrespect that you can't seem to let go of? You just don't want to stop because you know that God is calling you to step into that scary place of letting all that go, but continuing on in that sin just seems so much easier.

My friends...*follow Him.*

Follow Him into that spiritually scary place. That place that you don't want to go for whatever reason. Only you and God know the true reason why you don't want to go there. Yet He is beckoning to you anyway.

So let go of all your fears or your reasons and just *follow.*

When you learn to follow Him spiritually, then you will better be able to follow Him geographically, if that is His will for you.

Ever since I was little, I have wanted to follow Jesus wherever He led me. But I didn't want to just follow Him geographically, to Uganda one day. I wanted to follow Him into my own spiritually scary places.

Yeah, it's really hard. And sometimes it hurts as I have to let go of certain things or stretch out of my comfort zone.

But I want to do it anyway.

Will you?

Will you push through the hard times and through the pain and follow Him anyway? Will you let Him write your story?

If you've made it this far in this book, I think that you could be ready to say yes to each of those questions. And if you are, I am really proud of you. You are in for the adventure of a lifetime—one that you would never want to miss.

If you're not quite there yet that you want to say yes to those questions, it's okay. Pray about it and share with God how you are feeling. I do encourage you to realize that when God writes your story, things turn out so much better than you could have imagined.

You've come a long way throughout your reading of this book.

To be honest with you, the writing of this book was not always easy for me. At times I wanted to throw my laptop out the window and pull my hair out while screaming.

So I let God write with me. I let Him lay on my heart what He wanted me to share with all of you and I hope that it has encouraged you as much as it has encouraged me to write it. I'm learning a lot of these things with you. Like I said earlier, it's a dare we're taking together, remember?

So together let's take the dare to let God write our stories.

When you put this book down, I can almost guarantee you that the lies you stopped believing in chapter two, will slowly start to deceive you again. The fear you felt that you threw off in chapter three will start to creep in again.

Don't let it.

Don't believe those lies. Don't give into that fear.

If you choose to believe the truth and embrace your security in Christ, even when times are hard, you will be able to change your world. It's what God wants for you.

He's waiting for you, ready for you, to hand Him the pen of your life and then take a seat beside Him. He's just waiting to look into your eyes and tell you how much He loves you and how beautiful your life is to Him.

And then He'll start to write.

It may hurt and it may be uncomfortable.

But He'll write a beautiful story.

Oh, and about changing the world?

Well, you and God will do that together.

So go seek to know God deeper than ever before and learn to trust His bigger purpose. Go love unconditionally and believe in the impossible.

Don't you ever back down.

Decide to keep your eyes open and discover your passion. You never know what sort of beautiful legacy you will leave.

Let God write your story.

And go change your world.

*I dare you.*

"But what things were gain to me,
These I have counted loss for Christ.
Yet indeed I also count all things loss for the excellence of
the knowledge of Christ Jesus my Lord,
For whom I have suffered the loss of all things,
And count them as rubbish,
That I may gain Christ."

~Philippians 3:7-8~

# Appendix A

*A very long time ago* a Story greater than any other story we have ever heard began to unfold.

A Story of beauty, temptation, sin, danger, death, rescue, redemption, and most importantly...love.

This Story was like none other and it would change the world forever.

A Hero came down to a fallen world ravaged by sin and destruction to save a people that did not even know Him.

Death would be the only way to break the cycle of death and separation in the world and He would pay that costly price.

All for love.

Love that felt our pain and healed our hearts. Love that knew our temptation and provided an escape. Love that was so deep nothing could stop it...not even death.

We all long for it. That love that is so unconditional nothing can change it. A love that won't leave or desert you if you make a mistake. A love that will keep loving and being faithful, even when you are not. A love that only One can ultimately give us.

We search for it everywhere.

We search for it in our families, in our friends, in romance. We search for it in another person. We search for it in our dreams and in our hopes. We search for it in our jobs or in our money.

But nothing can satisfy that desire to be loved completely and unconditionally.

And yet we look at the Story told for centuries and choose to look past it or ignore it. We don't listen to the Story that could change our lives because we don't believe it.

But the best part of this Story is that it is *real*. It is a part of our history and it is a part of our lives. It is the love we long for so deeply but can never find.

You see, the Hero of our Story is Jesus Christ.

With a love that only Jesus could possess, He willingly became the Hero of our Story because it was the only way to save us. And as our Hero, He would have to give His life and die.

Jesus came to earth as a little baby, born in a humble stable, to give each and every one of us life. He lived a life of a true Hero, perfect and sinless. He taught, He healed, He changed lives.

And when the moment came for Him to lay down His life, He did it with you in mind.

Our Story changed a long time ago in a beautiful, perfect garden when one woman and one man decided to disobey God's plan and His instructions. This one act of disobedience changed everything forever. Separation from God was the cost. And there was no way for us to get back to Him on our own. We were lost until Jesus came. We have all sinned. We have all done our thing, gone our own way. No amount of good deeds would help us. No other ways could save us.

You may be hurting right now. You may not trust anyone. Everyone and everything you ever loved may have left you. Your heart may be shattered in pieces around you.

But even when everyone else leaves or hurts you, Jesus will always be right there to pick you back up, look into your eyes and tell you how much He loves you...

*"For God so loved the world that He gave His only begotten Son, that whoever believes in Him should not perish but have everlasting life. For God did not send His Son into the world to condemn the world, but that the world through Him might be saved."*

*~John 3:16-17*

*"For I am persuaded that neither death nor life, nor angels nor principalities nor powers, nor things present nor things to come, nor height nor depth, nor any other created thing, shall be able to separate us from the love of God which is in Christ Jesus our Lord."*

*~Romans 8:38-39*

*"But God demonstrates His own love toward us, in that while we were still sinners, Christ died for us."*

*~Romans 5:8*

*"For by grace you have been saved through faith, and that not of yourselves; it is the gift of God, not of works, lest anyone should boast."*

*~Ephesians 2:8-9*

*"In this the love of God was manifested toward us, that God has sent His only begotten Son into the world, that we might live through Him. In this is love, not that we loved God, but that He loved us and sent His Son to be the propitiation for our sins."*

*~1 John 4:9-10*

God's love is unconditional. He will love you no matter what. He will never leave you. His love will never stop.

Forgiveness for your sins is just a prayer away. God's arms are outstretched to you right now. The gap between you and God can be filled by His love for you if you just ask.

You don't have to do *anything* to earn His love. You can't do anything to earn His forgiveness. You don't need to earn redemption.

It is a gift and it is a gift that is being extended to you right this very moment.

*All you have to do is just believe.*

*Dear God, I know that I have sinned against You. I have broken Your perfect law. I have turned my back on You and I am sorry. Please forgive me. I believe that You sent Your perfect Son, Jesus, down to this world to die on the cross to save me and that He rose again on the third day. I believe, God.*
*I accept Your gift of forgiveness and redemption.*
*I accept Your love.*
*Thank You.*
*In Jesus' Name, Amen.*

*"But He was wounded for our transgressions, He was bruised for our iniquities; the chastisement for our peace was upon Him, and by His stripes we are healed. All we like sheep have gone astray; we have turned, every one, to his own way; And the Lord has laid on Him the iniquity of us all."*

*~Isaiah 53:5-6~*

# Appendix B

*Tips for Current and Future National Bible Bee Contestants* ☺

*I could not close out this book* without including this section for my Bible Bee friends, especially since I talked so much about Bible Bee throughout these pages!

Even if you have never done Bible Bee before, these tips I have also found are great for personal Bible study. Not to mention, I really think you should sign up for the Bible Bee. ☺

I have learned so much the past several years that I have done Bible Bee. I certainly know more about studying God's Word now than I did when I signed up for the local competition in 2011. God truly helped me in my study and memorization and I also owe so much to my many amazing Bible Bee friends for their helpful suggestions and tips.

First of all, I will share with you my studying tips. Over the years I have learned many!

## Study Tips:

My first study tip is to read the chosen book of the Bible over and over again...and then when you've finished reading it, read it again! The more times you read it, the more familiar it will become. I highly suggest memorizing that specific book of the Bible, as that is incredibly helpful for the written test. And the more times you read it, the easier memorizing it will be.

Next, I cannot encourage you enough to read commentaries! In 2013, the Bible book we studied for Nationals was Ephesians. There were some things in this book that were difficult to understand, so reading commentaries or listening to sermons on Ephesians was more helpful than I can say.

I also suggest that you buy a Greek lexicon/dictionary to have on hand at home.

Doing your own Greek (and Hebrew as well!) word studies is important for Bible Bee, but also for your own personal Bible study time. Learning Hebrew and Greek words can help you better understand the meanings of words in your Bible and it is a lot of fun once you get started!

For Bible Bee, familiarize yourself with the Greek/Hebrew words and definitions of several key words from the Bible book you are studying which will also prepare you for the written test.

I also began to write up summaries of the Bible books we were studying and cross-reference books. I gave titles to each chapter, summarizing what I learned. I did not begin doing this until the summer study of 2013. I quickly realized though how useful this is, especially for the National contest. This will help to trigger your memory about what a certain chapter was about which will help you immensely on the written test.

Just as you would write an outline for a school essay, write an outline for the Bible book you are studying. For those who hate doing outlines—like me—don't worry!

This is actually a pretty fun exercise and it really helped me dig deeper into the meaning of each chapter.

Whether you are participating in the local or national part of the competition, there will always be a lot of cross-references. If you want to see how the Bible fits together perfectly, looking up cross-references is really amazing.

During Bible Bee I began to study the context of the cross-references I found as well. I suggest reading the chapter or two around the verse you are studying. Let me give a quick example. Say you are looking up a cross-reference to *love* in 1 John 4 and you go to the cross-reference, John 3:16. To study the context, you could read all of chapter three, or even chapters two and four. This would give you an idea of who was speaking in this verse, why it was spoken, when it was spoken, and also surrounding conversations. This is also a good exercise to perform with your required memory passages. There are not that many required memory passages during the summer study, so it is often easier to do this for all of them then.

My final study tip is to have an accountability partner, preferably someone who is also doing Bible Bee. I cannot emphasize enough how immensely helpful it is to have so many friends from Bible Bee helping me as I study.

My first year doing Bible Bee, I did not know anyone else competing. That year I quickly learned the value of having a study partner who could give you advice and accountability. Try meeting with your accountability partner once a week to go over the things you are learning and any progress you may have made. If you are like me and all of your Bible Bee "family" lives in different states, then call or email each other once a week. ☺

*Memorization Tips:*

There is really nothing special about how I memorize verses. I normally just use rote memorization until I can quote the verses word perfect. This has always worked the best for me, but there are plenty of other ways to memorize.

Whatever your learning style may be, use it to help you memorize. Are you an auditory learner? If so, you probably learn best in school by hearing the lessons spoken to you. Whether you are memorizing on your own or for Bible Bee, have your accountability partner quote the verse over and over to you. Each time you could try saying it back. You could repeat this until you have it memorized. I used this method with my sister her first year doing Bible Bee. Usually you end up having a blast doing it together!

My brother however learns differently. He needs to hear me say it as well as read it himself. So I let him look at the memorization card while I read it aloud to him. You can tweak different memorization methods to whatever works best for you. It is really flexible and a lot of fun once you find the best way for you to memorize. If you want more tips on memorization for Bible Bee or just for your own memorization, I highly recommend reading, *The $100,000 Word* by Daniel Staddon. Daniel was the 1st place senior champion in the 2009 National Bible Bee and his book is very helpful.

A website I also use to help me memorize Scripture is www.memverse.com. Memverse is a lot of fun to use to memorize and also connect with others who are memorizing. I highly recommend it!

I now have a memorization tip specific to Bible Bee contestants. During the summer study before the local contest, we usually don't have very many required memory passages.

From personal experience, I recommend learning all the verses the first month of your study. By doing so, you will have more time to review them and perfect them. There will not be a scored oral test for locals, but it's still good to know them well for the written test.

For National qualifiers the amount of memory verses is usually a lot more. For 2013 Nationals, seniors were given 750 verses to memorize.

When I first found out that I was a national qualifier, I was beyond thrilled. Everyone in my church and down the street probably heard my excited screaming. I was so excited to begin studying, so as soon as I printed out my verse cards, I began memorizing. I memorized about 63 memory verses the first day and about 40 the next day. I memorized quite a lot the first few weeks and I am very glad I did. I highly recommend memorizing as many verses as you can when you are excited and ready for the challenge. As time goes on and it becomes a little bit harder, you will already have many verses memorized, giving you opportunities for a break if needed.

I also prefer to memorize the harder, longer verses first. Again, it is easier for me to do them in the beginning when I am excited and ready for the challenge. Then as the weeks go on, you will have shorter verses to memorize which will give you a welcome break.

## Testing Tips:

If you compete in the Bible Bee, you may feel some anxiety for the written test and oral test (if you are a national qualifier). During my first year at Nationals I was so nervous for the oral test that my voice was shaking as I quoted. As I continued to do Bible Bee each year, I learned some things that helped to keep my anxiety at bay. No, my nerves do not go away completely. I still feel nervous around competition day, but it's not as bad as it used to be.

First, it's just a test.

It is not a matter of life or death and if you don't know some questions or verses, that's okay. Allow yourself to make mistakes.

It's not the end of the world; trust me. My first year in the Bible Bee, I cried and was deeply distressed when I totally messed up my oral test. And when I say *totally*, I mean it. During my 2013 Nationals oral test, I totally messed up again. I had the lowest oral score I have ever received, but something was different this time. When I finished my test, I turned and smiled at my mom. I was disappointed, yes. But I realized that I should not be quoting the verses to get a perfect score. I was quoting them for the glory of Jesus Christ and it was okay with Him if I made a few mistakes.

If your focus is on worshiping and glorifying God through your testing, then you will be okay with yourself if you mess up. God taught me that, when we think we have totally messed up, He loves to surprise us so that we can give Him all the glory. He takes our ashes and turns them into beauty.

Coming out of my 2013 local written test, I thought for sure that I would not make the top 5 at my local contest and certainly not the national competition. God surprised me however and placed me 2nd at locals and 85th nationally. I was totally shocked and could only give glory to God alone.

If you still feel a little bit nervous, take a deep breath and just relax. Have fun taking your tests!

Local contest day and Nationals are my favorite days of the year because we have so much fun together! Just have fun quoting your verses for Jesus. He will be so proud of you. I just know it! Also, just enjoy being with your old friends and making new friends. Our friends are often the encouragement we need. I know that my friends were the ones to usually help keep me calm at Locals and Nationals.

Finally, don't focus on being timed. Knowing that you only have an hour for the written test can be a little intimidating, I know. But if you slow down and take your time, you have a better chance of scoring higher. Whenever I would rush through my practice tests, I would usually get questions wrong that I really knew the correct answer to. The time is not as bad as you think it is, especially if you are well prepared for the test.

Throughout the whole Bible Bee experience, the key is to give glory to God alone. Honor Him and remember that knowing Him is your reward. Knowing Him more deeply is worth everything we have to sacrifice and everything we have to do.

Before I close this section I would just like to say that if any of you participate in Bible Bee or are planning to, feel free to contact me. I'd love to know if you are planning on participating!

*"Therefore, whether you eat or drink, or whatever you do, do all to the glory of God."*

*~1 Corinthians 10:31~*

# Notes

[1] www.biblebee.org
*All information about the National Bible Bee in this book was written in late 2014. There have been changes to the competition since this was written, so please see their website for updated information.*

[2] Kevin Bales, *Disposable People* (Berkeley: University of California Press, 1999), p. 8. Bales researched and gave the most widely used estimate of slaves in the world today.

[3] Shayne Moore, Kimberly McOwen Yim. *Refuse to Do Nothing* (Downers Grove: InterVarsity Press, 2013), p. 30

[4] A21 Campaign website
<http://www.a21.org/content/human-trafficking/gl0ryw>
Accessed January 24, 2015

[5] UNICEF Factsheet: Child Soldiers
<http://www.unicef.org/emerg/files/childsoldiers.pdf>
Accessed January 24, 2015

[6] Charles Lavery, "Plight of African child slaves forced into mines—for our mobile phones." *Glasgow Sunday Mail* July 6, 2008. <http://www.laborrights.org/in-the-news/plight-african-child-slaves-forced-mines-our-mobile-phones> Accessed January 24, 2015

[7] If you go to www.slaveryfootprint.org, you have the opportunity to see how many slaves work for you based on the products in your home and you can do something about it by sending emails to companies, such as electronic companies like Microsoft, and food companies like Hershey's.

[8] To research more about child labor in the chocolate we consume visit: www.foodispower.org/slavery-chocolate/ Or visit: www.thedarksideofchocolate.org and watch the documentary *The Dark Side of Chocolate*.
You can also visit: www.fairtradeusa.org for more information about fairly traded products.

[9] You can visit Divine Chocolate's website at: www.divinechocolate.com

[10] You can visit Ben and Jerry's website at: www.benjerry.com

[11] For more information about these amazing organizations, you can visit their websites:
The International Justice Mission: www.ijm.org
Free the Slaves: www.freetheslaves.net
Not for Sale Campaign: www.notforsalecampaign.org
Hope for Justice: www.hopeforjustice.org
Love146: www.love146.org
A21 Campaign: www.thea21campaign.org
Restore International: www.restoreinternational.org

[12] A21 Campaign website: www.thea21campaign.org

[13] Abort73.com, "U.S. Abortion Statistics," <http://www.abort73.com/abortion_facts/us_abortion_statistics/> Accessed January 24, 2015

[14] American Life League, "Statistics: Abortions in the United States," <www.all.org> Accessed January 24, 2015

[15] American Life League, "Statistics: Abortions in the United States," <www.all.org> Accessed January 24, 2015

[16] Guttmacher Institute, "Induced Abortion in the United States," July 2014 <http://www.guttmacher.org/pubs/fb_induced_abortion.html> Accessed January 24, 2015

[17] For more information about these awesome organizations please visit their websites:
Rock for Life: www.rockforlife.org
Abort73: www.abort73.com
National Right to Life: www.nrlc.org
Save the Storks: www.savethestorks.com

[18] SOS Children's Villages USA, "Children's Statistics," <http://www.sos-usa.org/our-impact/childrens-statistics> Accessed January 24, 2015.

[19] SOS Children's Villages USA, "Children's Statistics," <http://www.sos-usa.org/our-impact/childrens-statistics> Accessed January 24, 2015.

[20] SOS Children's Villages USA, "Children's Statistics," <http://www.sos-usa.org/our-impact/childrens-statistics> Accessed January 24, 2015.

[21] For more information about these wonderful organizations, you can visit their websites at:
World Vision: www.worldvision.org
Amazima Ministries: www.amazima.org
Holt International: www.holtinternational.org
Compassion International: www.compassion.com

[22] For more information on Hoops of Hope go to: www.hoopsofhope.org

[23] For more information on these organizations, you can visit their websites:
National Suicide Prevention Lifeline: www.suicidepreventionlifeline.org
The Hopeline: www.thehopeline.com
To Write Love on Her Arms: www.twloha.com

[24] The book I read that day so long ago was called *Be The Change* by Zach Hunter. I highly recommend this book!

[25] Compassion International, "HIV/AIDS Facts," <http://www.compassion.com/poverty/facts-on-aids.htm> Accessed January 24, 2015

**All website addresses and phone numbers are current and accurate as of January 2015**

# Thank You...

First I must thank my precious Jesus. Where do I even begin, Lord? You are the One who gave me these words to write and share with the world. You are the One who placed Your dreams in my heart and dared me to do something with them. I love You and will be forever grateful for all You have done for me. You *died* for me! I can't even comprehend how much You love me and I cannot thank You enough. I will always follow You and I would give my life for You. You are ever faithful, my great God! You are *worth it all!*

Mom: Again, where do I begin? You are priceless to me and I will be forever thankful that God gave me you. Eight years ago you were the one to inspire me to start writing. Well, because of your encouragement I never stopped and here I am, eleven books later, with one published! Thank you for all you have done for me. I can't thank you enough. I love you beyond words.

Dad: Simply, thank you. For *everything*. But most importantly, thank you for being my dad even when you didn't have to be. When God brought you into my life when I was 13, I was blessed beyond measure! Thank you for the times you would spend in the living room listening to me read my book and talk about my dreams. Thank you for being the best. I love you, Daddy. Oh, and thank you for the Doritos. ☺

Kenzie: My sweet, "little" sister (five minutes always has counted!), you are a treasure beyond compare. I don't know where I would be without you. Thank you so much for encouraging me in the process of writing this book. You are truly an amazing writer and I hope to write as well as you one day! Thank you for daring me first. Now it's my turn: *I dare you to start your band and be a famous Christian rock star.* I love you, dear Kenzie!

Rylan: You are growing every day into the person God wants you to be. As I've watched you grow, I am happy to see how God has helped you in your life. Continue to let Him use you in this world. Thank you for being my brother and for listening at the dinner table those nights I would read my books aloud. I love you!

I have had so many wonderful friends encourage me as I have written. They have read my stories and have made me a better writer. They have encouraged me countless times. I would like to thank: Christine Holt, Hannah Murray, Courtney Minica, Ashley McMahan, and Kristi Elliott. You all feel like sisters to me and I love you very much!

There are so many other dear friends who have encouraged me to keep writing and doing something about my dreams as well, and I am thankful for each of you! I love you all so much!

Bethany: Thank you more than I can say. Thank you for letting me share your story in this book, but most importantly thank you for letting God use you to end slavery and make a difference in the world. Thank you for always being there for me no matter what and I know we will get to see each other soon! ☺ Keep changing the world, my dear "triplet"! I love you so much!

Thank you to all those who have encouraged me and helped me with Bible Bee over the years! I couldn't have done it without you! I would especially like to thank my pastor, Pastor David Rawley and his wife, Cindy. Thank you also to my youth pastor, Josh Lance and his wife, Abby.

Thank you to all of my amazing Bible Bee "family." You all have been such a blessing to me. One of the things I love about Bible Bee is that even though it is a competition, all of the contestants support and love one another. I love all of you, my Bible Bee friends, so much and thank you for all of the support and encouragement you have given me. You helped teach me so much.
Thank you to my Memverse friends as well.☺

Thank you to the team at CreateSpace who helped to make my dreams of being published come true.

Thank you to every single modern-day abolitionist out there who is fighting for justice and freedom. You all inspire me to use my voice and talents to make a difference. I have a deep respect for all of you. Especially to those who inspire me with the amazing organizations: International Justice Mission, A21 Campaign, Free the Slaves, Abolition International, Not for Sale Campaign, Restore International, the End It Movement, Love146, and so many others. May God bless you as you free the captives! You are all heroes!

And to Shannon Leary: You have inspired me so much. You are changing the world! Keep fighting injustice!

Thank you to the people who have inspired me in my dreams and encouraged me in my journey, even though they probably don't know it: Brittany and Tiffany Schlichter, Katie Davis, Christine Caine, Bob Goff, Zach Hunter, and Jen Ledger (you're amazing!). You all inspire me!

Thank you to my favorite band ever, Skillet. I don't know if you will ever see this or not. I want you to know that the *Rise* album was the inspiration behind a lot of this book. I thank you from the bottom of my heart and I love you all so much! You are making a big impact for Christ in this world. I can't wait for your next album! ☺

Thank you to all the many amazing, wonderful bands who played through my headphones during this writing process and encouraged me more than you will ever know!

And thank *you*, my readers. I have prayed for you as I have written this book and I continue to pray that the Lord blesses each of you as you pursue the dreams He has given you and as you change the world with them. So, just for fun, one last time (humor me): *I dare you to change your world for the glory of God.* Go out and do it! ☺

I'm sure I have probably forgotten to add someone here, and so I will apologize in advance! I truly am thankful for all of the wonderful people God has placed in my life during my journey. You are all loved very much and I can't say thank you enough!

May God bless each and every one of you! Much love to you all!

*Soli Deo Gloria!*
**Bella**

*"And Jesus came and spoke to them, saying, 'All authority has been given to Me in heaven and on earth.*
*Go therefore and make disciples of all the nations, baptizing them in the Name of the Father and of the Son and of the Holy Spirit, teaching them to observe all things that I have commanded you;*
*And lo, I am with you always, even to the end of the age.'*
*Amen."*

*~Matthew 28:18-20~*

# Mail-In Order Form

*Mail form and payment to:*
*Isabella Morganthal*
*P.O. Box 7*
*Burnt Cabins, PA*
*17215*

## I Dare You: Finding Your Passion and lighting Your World

### $12.99

Quantity: _____ ------------ Subtotal: _____

Shipping: *$3.00 first book, $1.00 per additional book* _____
*Check with the author for shipping rates outside of the United States.*

## The King's Princess Girl's Magazine Subscription

### $0.00

Your email address:

_____

TOTAL for ALL books: _____

**SHIP TO:**
NAME:

_____

ADDRESS:

_____

CITY: _____STATE: _____ZIP: _____